OUTLOOK AND PERSPECTIVES ON AMERICAN EDUCATION

Paul D. Houston

Published in partnership with the
American Association of School Administrators

ScarecrowEducation
Lanham, Maryland • Toronto • Oxford
2004

Published in partnership with
the American Association of School Administrators

Published in the United States of America
by ScarecrowEducation
An imprint of The Rowman & Littlefield Publishing Group, Inc.
4501 Forbes Boulevard, Suite 200, Lanham, Maryland 20706
www.scarecroweducation.com

PO Box 317
Oxford
OX2 9RU, UK

British Library Cataloguing in Publication Information Available

Library of Congress Cataloging-in-Publication Data

Houston, Paul.
    Outlook and perspectives on American education / Paul D. Houston.
        p. cm.
    "Published in partnership with the American Association of School
Administrators."
    ISBN 1-57886-071-7 (pbk. : alk. paper)
    1. School management and organization—United States. 2. Educational
leadership—United States. 3. Education—Aims and objectives—United
States. I. Title.
LB2805 .H696 2004
371.2'00973—dc21

                                                                    2003011869

⊗™ The paper used in this publication meets the minimum requirements of
American National Standard for Information Sciences—Permanence of Paper
for Printed Library Materials, ANSI/NISO Z39.48-1992.
Manufactured in the United States of America.

CONTENTS

INTRODUCTION

One of the great joys of my work as executive director of the American Association of School Administrators (AASA) these last few years has been the gift of having a "bully pulpit" to speak and write from. Anyone who knows me knows that I am not short of opinions or theories on nearly any subject. Also, anyone who knows me knows that I am passionate about certain things, among them public education, leadership, and the children served by education leaders. I also have my own views of education and how to make it better, and I am not easy on those simpleminded critics of education who think you can bludgeon people to greatness and who have simple answers to complex problems—those mechanics who would use a crowbar to heal a broken arm. Further, those who know me know that at my best moments I am creative and possess a unique insight into things, while at my worst I am just plain eccentric, random, and quirky. And, throughout it all, are words.

I was given the love of words by my father. He, too, spoke and wrote from a pulpit, but in his case it was a real one. When I was a child, he would play word games with me, and we would try to "outclever" each other with words. He and my mother are also responsible for the deep sense of spiritual connection I feel to the work that I do. I would hear him speak "the word" from his pulpit and came to understand the power of the word and the centrality of the spirit to our lives. So words, passion, anger, and a sense of spirit gush out of me like an artesian well pours forth water. I can't help myself.

Lucky for me, I have outlets for these. One main outlet has been a monthly column I've done for the *School Administrator*; I've also written guest articles in other journals.

My writing also reflects two of my other passions. It is a poorly kept secret that my real goal in life was to be a movie director. When I was a child, I was often asked if I wanted to be a minister when I grew up. Heavens no! I thought. Then I discovered later in life that the minister's pulpit I tried to avoid as a child was merely substituted for a larger and broader pulpit in public service to children. I also learned that my unfulfilled dream of directing movies was totally answered by the opportunity to direct real-life adventures with casts of thousands in school districts and associations. Nevertheless, my love of movies continues and appears often in my writing.

Although I was raised in the narrow confines of Davis Creek, West Virginia, I dreamed of the broader world and that someday I might have the chance to sample it. And I have. So far I have traveled to six continents and dozens of countries. I have visited classrooms from India to Indiana, and from California to Cuba. Most of these visits taught me a little about the place I was visiting and a lot about home. So I have used my travels to gain insights about us—what it is about America that is unique and worth preserving. And then there are the metaphors . . .

Growing up as a minister's kid in West Virginia, I was surrounded by stories, parables, and metaphors. They washed over me like the creek behind my house and became a part of how I see the world. As an adult I realize the real power in them is that they connect the listener and reader intellectually and emotionally and provide access to complex issues in understandable chunks. So I keep using them.

In the following pages, you will find my passions and theories spilling forth, along with insights from my travels, my time at the movies, and my "preaching" on how we might confound our critics, improve our work, and make the world a better place for our children. This book represents a part of my journey through the heart and soul of American education as we moved from the last millennium into this one.

Part I

ON BEING LEADER

I have always found it humorous that there are so many words for what we do—administrator, manager, superintendent, supervisor, head, CEO, and what have you—when one word and one thought would do: *leader*.

Of course, our concept of a leader tends to shape how we behave. If the metaphor is Patton, we go in one direction. If it is the Dalai Lama, we go in a very different one. The fact is that the world is thirsty for leadership. I have worried a lot about leadership over time. I have talked about it and I have written about it. What follows is a work still in progress, because leadership is a complex and changing concept. What passed for leadership thirty years ago wouldn't work today. What is successful in one context fails miserably in another.

What I have come to believe is that leadership has to do with our ability to follow and to place ourselves below those whom we are leading, and that we often move forward most effectively by stepping back and reflecting on what we are doing and why we are doing it. At its center, leadership is about moral purpose and remaining spiritually centered.

Certainly there are skills a leader needs. And today's leaders need skills that yesterday's leaders couldn't imagine. Butcher, baker, and candlestick maker have given way to spin doctor, piñata, and orchestra conductor. The following thought pieces begin to delve into what a leader in today's world is and must be able to do to succeed.

And through it all, leaders have to have balance—in our lives and between our heads and hearts. Balance will keep us upright and upstanding.

1

BALANCING PARADOX

The leader's art of finding satisfactory solutions by embracing two parts of a whole.

The role of leader in the modern organization is confusing and confounding. The landscape is littered with the bodies of CEOs who spent their professional lives successfully climbing the organizational ladder only to get to the top and find failure. Often this failure arises out of the ambiguity that is the life of a modern CEO.

Several years ago I had the good fortune to read a little book called *Management of the Absurd: The Paradoxes of Leadership* by Richard Farson. Farson outlines a number of paradoxes that confront leaders. My background was as a school superintendent, and the membership of the association I now run is made up of those folks, so I was naturally interested in Farson's views and sought him out. He said something that struck me as a fundamental truth: that if school superintendents were solving problems, then there was something wrong with their organizations, because problems that were solvable should have been solved prior to reaching the superintendent's desk. He went on to point out that the task of a superintendent is to mediate dilemmas—in essence to find the balance in paradox.

THE RIGHT TRADEOFFS

As I thought about that, I realized the irony that superintendents get to their positions by being good at solving problems. Then they reach the pinnacle of their profession only to find that the skills and knowledge that took them to the top are no longer valid. It wasn't the Peter Principle, which holds that in an organization people tend to rise to the level of their incompetence; they were still competent people. It was merely that people rise in the organization until they reach the role that calls for an entirely different set of skills than the ones that got them there.

Far too many leaders respond to the "dilemma of the dilemmas" by dropping back into the organization and solving other people's problems because that is their comfort zone. They feel better, but their staff is disempowered because the leader is doing the work that the staff should be doing. Or leaders close their doors and bang their heads on a wall because they have chosen a role that is so frustrating. Some leaders even create problems so that they can solve them. Most CEOs of complex organizations share the "dilemma of the dilemmas." Most issues that get to the top of an organization have no right or wrong answer—they present a spectrum with different tradeoffs. The role of a CEO is to find the right set of tradeoffs for the organization at that time and to feel comfortable knowing that it is OK not to know what the "right" answer is.

Precious little training exists to prepare people for the task of finding the right set of tradeoffs. Eastern philosophy, which embraces the idea of paradox, provides some guidance. Western thought tends to look at issues as black or white, right or wrong. Eastern thought recognizes that to every whole there are two parts, and that the prevalent conjunction is not *either or*; it is *and*. It is only by embracing both sides of the paradox that solutions and satisfaction arise.

With that in mind, I developed a set of paradoxes for leaders that I think will help the savvy CEO navigate his or her way between the rocks and through the rapids of modern leadership.

PARADOXES FOR LEADERS

Interdependent Autonomy

As a leader, you are alone in your decisions. The structure of organizations creates loneliness at the top, so autonomy is required. On the other hand, if you fail to recognize that modern organizations are interdependent ones in which symbiotic relations are critical, you're prone to fail. You must mesh your efforts with others. One of the ironies of school superintendency is that the key question you hear is, "What are you going to do about it?" People look to the leader to provide the answer. Yet no problem in a school system can be solved by the superintendent's absent significant collaboration with staff and often those outside the system.

Flexible Integrity

Effective leadership requires a moral center. You must consistently demonstrate a high level of integrity in thought, action, and decision. But if you are inflexible in your values and thoughts so that you cannot fit with the organization, and if you are unwilling to listen and, at times, to compromise, then you are apt to be rendered irrelevant. There is a thin line between integrity and dogmatism; people want their leaders to have a consistent moral compass, but be willing to alter directions if events demand it.

Confident Humility

The stresses of modern management will test your confidence to the breaking point. You must have a high level of personal fortitude and supreme confidence in your abilities, instincts, and values. But if you cannot match that confidence with an equally high level of humbleness, so that you are willing to listen to criticism and to act on new information, you'll be brought down by hubris. When I was superintendent of schools in Princeton, New Jersey, I used to joke that I had the easiest job in town. Everyone had a strong opinion of what I should do—the problem was, they wouldn't speak with one voice. The reality was that I had to have the personal confidence to move on issues as they arose, but I had to be humble enough to realize that there might be better ideas out there. This demands the skill of listening.

Cautious Risk-Taking

Leadership involves launching into uncharted waters. Otherwise, you and your organization will be doomed to hug the shore. But taking senseless risks can lead to a premature demise. It is good to know the capabilities of your boat and to be a seasoned sailor before you launch out into the unknown. Being cautious is prudent. Make haste, but do it carefully.

Bifocal Vision

Much has been made of late about the "vision thing," as one of our recent president's described it. Certainly, good leaders have to have their eyes on the horizon. They must demonstrate farsightedness. But if they lose their sense of the present and fail to attend to immediate details, they're likely to stumble over the rocks in the road long before they have a chance to reach the mountaintop. Leaders must be nearsighted as well. Good leaders must have a strategic approach to the job. As a superintendent, I had to know, in general, where the system needed to be several years in advance. Many of my decisions and actions had to lead to those goals. Yet I was also acutely aware that I needed to make good "snow day" decisions (those pesky calls superintendents have to make at 4 a.m.) so that I could maintain my credibility to keep the job and the momentum necessary to get us where we needed to go. Leaders need a lens that accounts for both far and near.

Wobbly Steadiness

People in organizations have to know where the leader stands. A leader must convey steadiness of purpose and a consistent style to give folks a sense of stability and constancy. But if the leader can't alter course as conditions and reality shift, the organization will run aground. The course must be a steady one, but with a good deal of play and side-to-side maneuvering to avoid the obstacles and to get around the problems. It's much like the proverbial ant making its way toward the picnic basket. Its goal is clearly in mind, even as it avoids rocks and branches that lie in its path.

Skeptical Beliefs

Leaders must have a firmly established set of beliefs that guides their decisions and actions. Good leaders lead from the inside out. Yet good leaders must constantly remain skeptical—especially of themselves. If you are closed or hardheaded about your beliefs, you will become rigid and incapable of change. As the world changes, so must the framework.

Thick-Skinned Empathy

Leaders often serve as lightning rods. Leaders are ground zero for pressure and criticism. You must be strong enough to take a punch. But if the fire hardens you, you'll lose that part of your humanity that is critical to leadership. You must maintain the ability to feel with those you lead. Leaders in any organization tend to have a public face and are subject to second-guessing and criticism. My role as a school superintendent gave me the opportunity to hear about my decisions on talk radio, read letters to the editor about my performance, see caricatures of myself in editorial cartoons, and hear personal vilification in public meetings. This meant that my personal confidence level had to be pretty high. Yet as a leader of thousands of adults who are responsible for the futures of thousands more children, I needed to "feel others' pain" and to relate to their needs. If your shell gets too hardened through the desire for survival, it will ultimately be an empty shell.

Lowly Aloofness

Leaders must always stand on high ground. That gives the best view of the battlefield. You cannot afford to get pulled into the fray where things are down and dirty. While standing on high ground allows you to see across the distance, you cannot afford to distance yourself from your followers. Leaders are only useful if they take the followers to the mountaintop, too. That means putting your followers above yourself—the essence of the servant leader.

Childlike Maturity

Effective leaders must show remarkable maturity. They can't take things personally. They exhibit calm in calamity and grace under pressure. Good leaders must provide the adult supervision that organizations require. But great leaders also retain the innocence and wonder of children. They delight in the unexpected and see the world not as a thing to be conquered but as a journey to be enjoyed. They keep a place in their hearts for the possibility that the tooth fairy and Santa Claus (or at least their spirits) do exist. Good leaders stay in touch with their inner child.

If leaders come to understand that their roles are confounding because life is made up of opposites that create tension, they can confront their roles

more realistically. And if they come to understand that these apparent con-
tradictions also create balance, then they can embrace the task of leading
with a sense of possibility and joy.

2

SUPERINTENDENTS FOR THE TWENTY-FIRST CENTURY

It's Not Just a Job, It's a Calling

I once had a school board president who told me that my job as a superintendent was to be a quick-healing dartboard. And he was a supporter of mine! Over the years I have used a number of other metaphors to describe the role, all of them just about as unappealing. I get the greatest response when I say that the relationship of the superintendent to the community is analogous to that of a fire hydrant to a dog. The reality of the modern superintendency is that it is both exciting and exasperating, and we are finding it increasingly difficult to attract people to the role. Understandably, people don't want to be dartboards or fire hydrants. As we face the challenges of a new century, we must find ways to reconfigure the role of the superintendent so that it attracts our best leaders, even as we also transform it to meet the opportunities that change presents.

There are a number of reasons people are not interested in becoming superintendents. They see the "lightning rod" aspect of the job, and they choose not to do it. The superintendency is a job fraught with public criticism and mixed with private moments of triumph. Superintendents are sometimes abused and other times blamed. Expectations are high and often unrealistic. I have frequently thought that, if I ever wrote a book on the subject, I would call it *What Are You Going to Do about It?* That phrase sums up the almost universal expectation that somehow one person in an organization can shoulder the responsibility for all aspects of the organization. That person must provide the "final answer." But, unlike contestants sitting opposite Regis Philbin, superintendents are given no lifelines to help with questions that seem to have no answers.

Yet, when superintendents get together, after they vent about their problems, they tend to talk mostly about their successes. And many who leave the job find themselves working their way back into it. While the job is fraught with external pressures, it is filled with internal possibilities. Superintendents know they can change the trajectory of children's lives, alter the behavior of organizations, and expand the possibilities of whole communities. This creates a powerful attraction to the job. Such ambivalence makes the superintendency a wonderful subject of study. As education stands in the national spotlight, there are few roles as complex or as pivotal as that of the public school superintendent. And as we move into the future, it is inevitable that the job will continue to be one of controversy, concern, and consequence.

Most of the people who have been superintendents have found it exhilarating and challenging in the best sense of that word. It is clearly a position in which a person can make a big difference. But there is much about the current role that is dysfunctional. Expectations and resources are mismatched. Accountability and authority are misaligned. This means there must be a shift in expectations and a corresponding shift in role. Part of the shift that must take place is a change in how the world sees and treats superintendents. But the bigger part of the shift must take place in the hearts and minds of those who fill the role. For how one chooses to confront the challenges of the superintendency will make all the difference.

As a minister's son, I realized early in my own career as a superintendent that there are a great many spiritual overtones to the superintendency. The ultimate responsibility of the role is to shepherd other people's children through the often dangerous valley of childhood. So it is easy to see religious symbolism in the role. That led me to a realization that superintendents tend to spend most of their careers between Palm Sunday and Good Friday. They enter a community as a new savior who is thought capable of performing miracles and healings. Sometime later, they are put on trial, marched through the streets in public humiliation, and crucified. Jonathan Kozol once said that he thought that cities needed superintendents because they needed someone to die for their sins. While this is a disturbing thought, there is still the reality that Easter Sunday follows Good Friday and that resurrection remains possible. The superintendent of the twenty-first century must look to the hope of resurrection as the source of possibilities for success. It is a tough job, but it is one that bears great promise and possibility.

THE CHALLENGES

While much of the attention of school reformers is focused on accountability, test scores, standards, and the like, much of the superintendent's job is actually shaped by issues that exist on a more macro level. And that is where the superintendent of the twenty-first century should focus attention.

School leaders of every stripe must face a number of broad social challenges that are reshaping our society and the way children learn. These are what I call the "demanding Ds" of change that will shape the future. They are things like changing *demographics* and growing *diversity*. The shift in population to Sunbelt states, the generational divides created by baby booms and baby busts, and the changing complexion and accent of America's children all create real challenges for school leaders.

The job is made more difficult by the *divide* between the haves and have-nots and by the *devaluing* of our children. The dirty little secret of American education is the degree to which we allow inequities in resources to exist between communities. These inequities mean that the children with the greatest need often have the fewest resources, and that those who come to school as the most advantaged are given even more support once they enter the schoolhouse door. Although America leads the world in talking about how much it values its children, it is often near the bottom of developed countries in the measures that show how it truly values its children. That is because America tends to put its resources into remediation rather than prevention. This was best summarized for me by someone who pointed out that America is a nation that will air-condition its prisons but not its schools.

One cannot overlook the *de-emphasis* on education that leads us to substitute test scores for learning and to believe that the only goal of education is making a living rather than making a life. But there are several Ds that strike directly at the heart of what the superintendent of the future will do.

The first of these is *deregulation*. Most major industries in the United States have been deregulated, and it is now education's turn. This change manifests itself in such issues as homeschooling, vouchers, and charter schools, as well as in the massive changes brought on by privatization. The reality is that the world for a twenty-first-century school leader will be one in which competition is a way of life and scrambling for dollars and customers will be requisites for the job. The role of the future will not merely entail running a school system. The superintendent of the future will also serve as a broker of services and as an ensurer of equity. The task will be to determine which services are needed and what the best source of the services is and then to make sure that every child benefits from them.

The second big issue confronting school leaders is *devolution*. This is the historical wave that pushes power from centralized to decentralized places. It was the force behind the breakup of the countries in Eastern Europe, it is the force behind the growth in power of America's governors, and it is the force behind the movement toward site-based management in America's schools. What are the implications for people who have traditionally run centralized organizations, such as school systems, in a devolutionary moment of history? Successful superintendents of the twenty-first century will be those who find a way of leading by sharing power and by engaging members of the organization and the community in the process of leading.

The third big issue that directly affects superintendents is *demassification*. Historically, people got their information from mass media that were limited in diversity. When I grew up, I had three choices of television channels to watch. Today's children have literally hundreds. This increase in choice is both positive and popular. People can choose how they spend their time and to whom they are exposed while they spend it. However, it also means there are fewer common experiences that hold society together, and this erosion of the common ground necessary to hold a democracy together presents a potential threat to our future.

Although the experience of public schooling still constitutes much of that common ground, the very institution of public education is increasingly being called into question. The challenge to public education created by the nearly twenty years of unrelenting criticism of schools presents a clouded future. What happens to America if the movement toward demassification destroys the ties that bind? Superintendents of the future must focus on creating learning for children that is on the one hand individualized and connected to personal interests and on the other hand inclusive of the broader social context that will allow children to live together in our increasingly complex democracy.

The final issue that will have profound implications for school leaders is *disintermediation*. This daunting word refers to a phenomenon that occurs when a technology introduced into society replaces old institutions. For example, when Gutenberg invented the printing press and in so doing made the Bible accessible to the masses, he "disintermediated" the church. People no longer had to go to a priest to get the interpretation of God's will. They could read and decide for themselves. That led to the Reformation and a profound shift in humanity's relationship to God.

Today, computers, CDs, and the Internet are disintermediating schools. Schools have been the place where people go to get learning. That is no longer necessarily true. Parents and children no longer have to go to school to have access to skills or knowledge. They can access these via technology. What are the implications for leaders in this brave new world? Twenty-first-century superintendents will understand that learning is no longer about place, it is now about process. They will find ways of extending the reach of schools beyond the schoolhouse door, while maintaining the traditional and historic role of public schools as central to our society. Schooling must continue to convey civic virtue to our population.

We can like or dislike these challenges. It doesn't matter. They are with us, and that is really all that counts. How school leaders choose to face them will make the difference in how the future looks. And choosing to face this new future from a position of strength will require a new breed of leader.

A SUPERINTENDENT OF EDUCATION

The reality is that, for superintendents to be successful in the future, they will need to completely change their approach to the job. Historically, if superintendents were good at the management issues, they were held to be successful.

Let's call that being good at the "killer Bs." These were things like buildings, buses, books, budgets, and bonds. It was the "stuff" of education. A superintendent was a superintendent of schools, with the presumption that school was a place for learning and that the superintendent's job was to take care of that place. The future dictates a very different approach.

Educators are fond of pointing out that it takes a village to raise a child. But this begs a crucial question—what does it take to raise a village? We are

no longer a country of villages, and the web of support that historically supported families and children is tattered. It must be rewoven, and the superintendent must play a pivotal role in that task. Superintendents of the future
must see themselves as village builders. They can use the centrality of their
institutions to help re-create a support system. But they must do so by reaching outward to connect to the resources of the broader community.

That means they will have to be masters of the "crucial Cs." The Cs are
the processes that support the work and get it done. They are things like
connection, communication, collaboration, community building, child advocacy, and curricular choices.

Leadership in the future will be about the creation and maintenance of relationships: the relationships of children to learning, children to children,
children to adults, adults to adults, and school to community. The increasing
complexity of our society, the deterioration of families, and the loss of social
capital available to support children and families mean that superintendents
must be adept at creating a web of support around children and their families.
School leaders can no longer wait until a child is five years old to become involved with his or her learning. Much research has demonstrated that the
early years of a child's life are crucial. If schools wait to address a child's needs
past those formative years, the subsequent work becomes much more difficult.

Leaders cannot forget about children after 3 p.m. Children spend the
bulk of their time someplace other than school. If schools are not helping to
shape that time through parent education and after-school and summer
learning opportunities, the work that schools do will be diluted. Schools
must become part of the broader social context that creates a true system of
lifelong learning in the community. This does not mean that schools must
become all things to all people. It means schools must team up with other
caregiving agencies, such as the health department, the parks and recreation
folks, or the church down the street to see to it that a network of mutual care
is created around the children and their families.

Creating this network will require skills that differ from those traditionally
used by superintendents. The ability to communicate and to market ideas
will be critical. Superintendents in the twenty-first century will need to be
able to facilitate and affiliate. They will need to turn in their "power over"
skills of command and control and take on a "power with" mentality that al

lows everyone to be part of the action. This is a huge shift in perception and approach, for which new training models will be needed.

The key point is that we will no longer be able to pretend that learning stops and starts at the schoolhouse door. Learning has always been affected by the contextual issues that plague many children and families, and the superintendents of the twenty-first century must become courageous champions for children, using their skills to muster the broad support for children and families that will enable children to be successful at learning.

But superintendents will need to do more. They will also have to be leaders who see that the content of learning changes dramatically. Yes, they will have to create conditions that get children ready for school. But they will also have to create conditions that get schools ready for children.

NEW APPROACHES TO LEARNING

Critics of education have argued for some time that our current system is a failed system, a system that has deteriorated over time and must be reenergized and reshaped by competition if it is to recapture its past glory. This is a false reading of history. The reality is that the current system is better than ever at conducting its historic mission. The problem is that, while the system has gradually improved, conditions have exploded around it. Schools have been making incremental progress in an exponential environment. That does mean that major transformation is required—not because the system has failed, but because the mission has shifted.

The recognition that we must transform the system has led us to the current efforts at school reform. Unfortunately, these reforms are based on a faulty analysis of what ails us. If you lean your ladder against the wrong wall, you will paint the wrong house. If you believe that the problem of American education is that we need to *force* students to learn by giving them high-stakes tests and a narrow curriculum, then you will create our current model of reform—a model that is doomed to failure. It is doomed because current reform efforts are external and overly simplistic. Those who endorse these current reforms rely on the belief that you can bludgeon people to greatness through external pressure. Their efforts are built on a mechanistic worldview that stresses fixing the parts to create a better whole.

Education, however, is a human enterprise. So the solution to its problems must be much more organic. It must recognize that all parts of the system are interwoven and that moving one affects all the others. In essence, the difference between current reform efforts and what is truly needed to change schools for the twenty-first century is the difference between geology and ecology. Geology gets its power by studying the past layers of rock that envelop the earth. It is a somewhat fixed science that gains its power by studying inert objects. Ecology recognizes the existence of ecosystems—interconnected systems of living organisms—that are highly interdependent. The slightest change in one affects all the others. That is also true of the education system.

These differing perspectives on reform lead to very different assumptions about how learning happens. One assumes that learning is external and can be invoked from without. The accountability and competition movements are based on this belief system. Those who hold this view forget that education and learning are essentially internal and tied directly to motivation. Education is really about evocation—drawing forth the creation of meaning from the learner. Fear has never been a particularly effective motivational tool, particularly when complex thought processes are required. That means that reforms built on a foundation of fear are doomed.

Thus effective school reform in the future will focus on creating schools that students want to go to. These schools will have to be places that are engaging and that allow learners to undertake activities they find meaningful. Creating such schools will require a total revamping of how we approach teaching and learning, and it will require leaders who are focused on the process. Twenty-first-century superintendents will have to be leaders who focus on the organic and holistic qualities of learning and who structure learning that speaks to the hearts and minds of learners.

Creating such schools will require opening them to the broader world. Meaningful learning can happen only in the broadest possible context. Once again, the future will require leaders to turn the current process inside out and to structure learning so that students will use complex skills in practical situations that challenge their thinking while connecting them to reality. It's a tall order.

WHO WILL THESE LEADERS BE?

How will we find leaders who can act as courageous champions for children and who are willing and able to change the status quo, while acting as collaborative catalysts and working with others to make that happen? We must look very hard to find a source for such leaders. There are really just four problems with the current leadership system: the job is impossible, the expectations are inappropriate, the training is inadequate, and the pipeline is inverted.

The job is impossible because the expectations are unrealistic. We want one individual to be all and know all in a complex system. Furthermore, while we tend to centralize responsibility in education, authority is widely dispersed. We ask superintendents what they are going to do about a particular matter, while we spread the power to do something across a system that includes boards, unions, and community groups. Of late, governors, legislators, and judges have also taken a bite out of the authority apple.

With the current emphasis on accountability, the problem intensifies. Accountability without authority is punishment. That means that either authority must be recentralized—unlikely in a world of devolution and demassification—or responsibility must be decentralized. That means that we must evolve a distributed system of leadership in which the skills and the ability to make things happen and the accountability for whether they did happen are spread across a wider spectrum. Under this model, the superintendent must be a team leader and team developer.

Our current training system is inadequate for this new model, because it reflects a rearview mirror approach to leadership. Most of the coursework now required for licensure focuses on the old role. It prepares people for centralized, command-and-control managerial tasks. It doesn't teach the collaborative skills needed in today's more complex and connected environment.

Superintendents must be great communicators. They must be outstanding facilitators. They have to know how to take the pulse of the public and how to sell their ideas. Persuasion is the ultimate tool for a superintendent of education. This is particularly true when dealing with boards of education. The disconnect between superintendents and boards has become almost the stuff of legend, and there are no quick fixes to the problem. However, one thing that would help would be to offer superintendents better preparation for working in a collaborative way with their boards. Leadership in this arena isn't about exerting the superintendent's will but about working collaboratively with a board for the greater good.

And certainly our current training fails to recognize that leadership in the future will be all about navigating white water. When you get to the top of the organization, there are no right or wrong answers. There are merely dilemmas. There are paradoxes, with each option having both good and bad implications. How does one prepare leaders for such choices?

First, we must recognize that this is reality. We must help our leaders let go of the "black and white" mindset that sees the world as an "either/or" kind of place and come to understand that it is really a "both/and" place, where both ends of the continuum can hold equal elements of truth.

The best training for this would be cross-disciplinary and embedded within preparation for becoming a reflective practitioner. Since the role is being shaped by pressures outside of education, school leaders must be aware of and knowledgeable about these pressures. This means they must be historians, demographers, sociologists, and futurists. And because the work is centered on and carried out by people, management ideas from the business school and spiritual awareness found in the divinity school would also be appropriate.

Of course, nothing about leadership in a fast-paced, pressurized environment encourages reflection. In fact, everything about the superintendent's role makes it reactive rather than reflective. Yet seeing the whole can come only in moments of quiet contemplation. This necessitates forcing reflection onto an active leader. It won't be easy, but it can be done. It comes about through the experiences of writing journals, mentoring, and teaching. Much of the coursework in superintendents' preparation should concentrate on problem analysis. Preparation programs for the next generation of leaders must involve a constant dance between doing the work and thinking about it. Over time, doing this will produce a reflective practitioner.

The current pipeline into school administration is inverted. There are many people in it who have great potential for leadership. They must be nurtured and encouraged. But the profession can no longer depend solely on those who choose it—that is, the "wannabes." We must begin to identify a new cadre of leaders who see the role as one of collaboration, rather than of command, and then mentor them into the jobs. These are the "oughtabes," and they must be identified and encouraged. The good news is that the pipeline is filled with them. Nearly two thirds of the current staff members in district offices are women, and many of them have mastered the skills of affiliation and collaboration through the process of acculturation that we seem to reserve for little girls. We must find ways of shattering the remnants of the glass ceiling and making the role attractive to this new kind of leader.

A MISSION, NOT A JOB

This brings me back to the central question of why anyone would want to do these jobs. Superficially, the current role isn't very attractive, and the challenges we can see for the future make it potentially even more difficult. Why would anyone in his or her right mind choose to become a dartboard or a fire hydrant? What kind of job is that?

It is, in fact, a very challenging job with many frustrations and perils. It is also a job with many psychic rewards. Superintendents have the chance to reshape the lives of children in profound ways. They can create a sense of community where none exists. They can transform institutions of learning through their leadership and courage. They can make smooth the rough path.

I once heard Cornel West, a Harvard professor, describe the superintendency as "soul craft." And he was right. School leadership is about the mind and about how we might better shape the minds of our children. But it is also about touching hearts. And that makes the work much more sacred than we have traditionally thought.

It is ironic that education has become embroiled in the battles over the separation of church and state, when so much of what we do in education is akin to the work of the churches. School leadership focuses on the substance of what it means to be a human and to live together harmoniously in this world. Education isn't about the skills we teach, it is about the spirits we nurture. For without healthy spirits, the world is full of young people like Eric Harris and Dylan Klebold who could grow into Fidel Castros and Adolf Hitlers.

St. Francis of Assisi once said that if you work with your hands, you are a laborer. If you work with your hands and your head, you are a craftsman. But if you work with your hands, your head, your heart, and your soul, you are an artist. School leaders will be effective only if they choose to be artists.

School superintendents like to see themselves as CEOs, for they are responsible for the entire school organization. But with authority so widely distributed, that is not an effective model. Certainly, superintendents have the responsibility of CEOs, but they lack the authority. A better analogy might be to liken themselves to ministers. Ministers get their authority from on high. When you work with other people's children and become responsible for them, that is very powerful moral authority. Moreover, ministers get their work done by means of persuasion and by creating common purpose. That is really the challenge of the superintendent of the future. Can we find ways of bringing communities together in a kaleidoscopic environment to create a better world for our children?

The superintendency isn't so much a job as it is a calling. You may choose it, but it also chooses you. You are summoned to it. Part of the responsibility of the current generation of leaders will be to summon that next generation to duty. And that leads back to the fire hydrant. Yes, the hydrant does serve as a convenience for the dog, but that isn't its mission. Its mission is a much more noble one. It is there to keep houses from burning down. Public school leaders may get a little damp from time to time from the exercises of their critics, but their mission is to help children create a future where democracy is preserved and the ideals of this nation are moved forward. And that is a wonderful challenge and an amazing gift to receive.

3

THE PUBLIC'S
RIGHT TO GNAW

Iam amazed that educational leaders don't all look like an anorexic Ally McBeal on a really thin day. They are dined upon regularly by the public as they are served up in the press. In this one corner of our society, cannibalism not only is accepted, it is encouraged through public feasting.

Now don't misunderstand. I believe in a free press and I believe in the public's right to know how its tax-supported institutions are run. School leaders must cooperate with the press. The public does have a right to know. However, that has its limits, and those limits are when the knowing becomes gnawing.

Most of us are familiar with "board watchers." These folks turn up at every school board meeting hoping a good fight breaks out. I always wondered if they were good citizens, incipient sadists, or just folks who couldn't afford cable television and needed to find their entertainment elsewhere. I just knew I was there because I *had* to be—not because I thought it was the best show in town.

Of course, the other group required to be in attendance besides the school board and staff was the news media. Sometimes I wonder if the bad press received by public schools comes about because the reporter seeks revenge for having to sit through meetings that rarely rise above the level of intense tedium.

I do believe school systems would be better served if the press were to handle their awesome responsibility a bit more responsibly. I am not talking here about the occasional misquote or twisted story. Generally, reporters are well intentioned and are not out to zing us. The problem stems from the decisions of what editors and news directors define as news, and whether the public's best interest is served by those decisions.

OVERBLOWN COVERAGE

There are several areas of coverage that I think have hurt schools and have not really served the public's needs. The first is the coverage of violence. Clearly, when an act of violence occurs in a school, it is news. Yet, often, these incidents are covered well out of proportion to the actual number of incidents, or the school gets tied to something that is bigger than the school. I remember stories about murder victims who were found near school X. The murder had no connection to the school beyond the geography of the victim's demise. Or the murderer who, when caught as a forty-year-old, is shown to have attended school Y. Why isn't the church or synagogue they attended or the clubs they belonged to seen as equally relevant to the present circumstances?

Of course, the school shootings of the past several years have become a cottage industry. Too rarely are these events tied to the bigger picture. There have been shootings in the workplace, restaurants, day care centers, and churches. They all deserve examination so they won't happen again. Looking at only a part of the picture will not yield a clear solution.

While the initial story is newsworthy, many follow-up stories are not. When is enough enough? Also, a little context would be good. It is awful that children are shot in school. Each year twenty or thirty students are killed in school. Each year we lose several thousand young people to shootings at home or in public places. Where are they safest? Focusing on the exception yields exceptionally poor analysis of the real problems.

For similar reasons, the media's incomplete reporting of test scores through the ranking of schools without the information on the differences in social capital available to kids distorts the picture. This has driven a lot of state and national policy and has led to poor decisions being made about how best to solve school problems. That is like rank ordering hospitals based on a report of the number of cancer cases in each as a way of creating a cure. More needs to be told and understood.

We also saw a proliferation of stories on homeschooling when home-schooled kids won the national spelling bee. Trying to draw systemic comparisons based on individual accomplishments is even more naive than thinking that a kid who can spell *naiveté* is well educated. It is important to remember two things: the sum is always greater than a single part, and the spell-checking function for personal computers was invented so we wouldn't have to memorize lists of rarely used words.

MESSAGE MANAGEMENT

Finally, let's think about what the open public meeting law has done to board/superintendent relations. How can we have an open, honest discussion of differences in public? It is the rare board that can pull that off. More likely what is seen in public is preening and posturing. An honest discussion of differences that can be made in private becomes a platform for bad behavior in public. I am not suggesting that everything belongs in private. But school board self-examinations and retreats on working together deserve the respect that privacy offers.

Not to let you think I am letting school leaders off the hook here, let me end by pointing out that most of what I have been ranting about thus far is not likely to change in our lifetime. So the answer falls squarely on the backs of school leaders to become more adept at dealing with the public and its right to know. We must develop better skills at shaping our stories and getting them out. We must find alternate ways of getting information to the public. And we must take responsibility for being the message managers of our districts. That will require a new set of skills and attitudes. But anything short of that will mean that we are going to be the public's super-sized meal as they chew on our foibles and failures.

4

REFILLING THE WELL

Have you ever noticed that no one comes into your office to bring you things? They come seeking something. They want your time, your energy, your permission, your wisdom, or your resources. They come to you out of the need to dip their bucket in your well and to drink from your spring, and that is how it should be. That is the role of leader—to serve others. But there is a danger.

What happens when your well goes dry? For if all that you do is give, then, at some point, you will have nothing left to offer. That is when burnout (or should I say "dry-up") occurs. That is the time when you wonder why you are doing what you are doing, and when your sense of satisfaction follows the full buckets out your door. There is an antidote. Make sure your own well stays filled.

The challenge is that you must be the one to keep it full. This means that you must develop your own plan for bringing balance to your life. Several years ago AASA created a strand at the National Conference on Education that focused on creating balance. It was recognition that a successful leader must be a successful human being, and being a successful human requires a balance among the head, the heart, and the body.

A successful educational leader must have a rich intellectual life. I have sometimes joked that school leaders don't read. The truth is that they read what they have to read, and that tends to leave little time for what they should read. That means they need to create their own opportunity to read and study outside the field of education.

SUMMER ENRICHMENT

One of my favorite weeks each year is the week I spend cohosting the Harvard Seminar for Superintendents. It is a good experience because it combines the opportunity for colleagues to meet and to share ideas, war stories, and moral support with a rich intellectual experience. The content of the program is provided by the Harvard faculty. The one requirement is that their lectures not be about education.

Of course, the participants spend the entire week trying to figure out what developing a cure for cancer or the unfinished works of Mozart has to do with their work as school leaders. This creates an intellectual curiosity and creativity that, I am convinced, makes them better leaders when they go home. Tip number one for refilling the well: Read and read broadly.

Sadly, most educators spend so much time in their heads that they neglect the rest of their bodies. Some of our more obsessive colleagues are avid runners or bikers. But most of us get our exercise running for cover at school board meetings. A regular program of exercise will keep us better able to meet the challenges and increase our longevity, but it also makes us more productive. The mind is clearer and more active when the body is also. Tip number two: Develop a regular program of exercise that fits your lifestyle and fitness level. And stick to it.

The Greeks understood the concept of "keeping the well full." They spoke often of maintaining a balance of "sound mind and sound body." When I visited Greece a few years ago, I realized they placed a theater next to a stadium so that architecturally they were living out their dictum. But there was a third element and a third edifice in the complex—a temple. For it is not enough to feed the mind and body if we starve the soul.

A SPIRITUAL AWARENESS

We have been reminded that we are not human beings having a spiritual experience, but we are spiritual beings having a human experience. For the last few years, I have tried to incorporate the issue of spiritual life into my speeches. I did so initially with some trepidation. We are, after all, stewards of public schools and as such must be mindful of the separation of church and state.

But having a spiritual life is not the same as proselytizing for a specific religion. Being in touch with our spiritual self is critical to leadership. We are responsible for others' children and, in many ways, for the future of this country. We had better be connected to our highest selves and purpose, or we are apt to lose our way very quickly. Tip number three for keeping the well filled: Find a way to connect to the heart and soul within you, for that is the path to serenity.

Anyone who has tried leadership knows that it is hard under the best of circumstances. School leadership isn't for the faint of heart. And servant leadership, which is the only true leadership, takes much from the one giving it. While there is always a psychic exchange in every human interaction, servant leadership takes ideas, energy, and balance from the one acting as leader in exchange for knowing one is doing good.

That exchange is a fair one, but to keep giving ideas and energy, one must refill the well to supply those things. It won't happen naturally. Humans are not artesian springs with boundless supplies of creativity, vitality, and dreams. Keep the well filled and the fountain flowing by maintaining a balance among the head, the heart, and the soul.

5

TRANSFORMATION
Abandoning Command, Control

In 1998, I ran across a report from the National Education Association's National Center for Innovation Learning Laboratory Initiative on leadership and school change. It pointed out that "leadership is a constantly distributed commodity." As such, the report called into question the popular notion that principal leadership is crucial for school change. The report basically said that it all depends on style and approach. Nothing earthshaking here. What would you expect a teachers' organization to say? However, I was most interested to find that while principal leadership is not required for school change, "superintendent leadership is basic to transformational change."

The report went on to state that "changes in few other places in school districts can influence the presence or pace of transformational change like the superintendency." These leaders tend to establish systems and processes that eventually do not require their presence at all. Successful change, in fact, should outlive the superintendent.

Central offices are another story. They tend to dominate the culture of schools. They control, despite the perception that control resides with more visible leaders. They tend to enforce conformity. Therefore, they do not lead and might inhibit transformational change.

One of the major tasks for a superintendent is to see that central offices create capacity for change in the organization and do not act as brakes on progress. To do so will require major organizational transformation, from a bureaucratic model of command and control to an effort at nurturing and supporting.

The transformation of district offices must be a distinct movement from where we are to where we need to go. Fundamentally, it should move a district from operating on fear to operating on trust. Districts cannot assume that schools, principals, and teachers will try their best to do their worst. If you expect the worst from people, you will not be disappointed—you'll get it. So the underlying emotion that a superintendent must take to the task is trust. He or she must expect that the district office will begin treating staff as the adults they are and need to be.

District offices must be moved from demanding compliance to fostering creativity. There is something wrong with a system that offers forgiveness easier than it does permission. Such a system encourages outlaw behavior on the part of staff. District offices must find ways of moving from rules and regulations, which give a whack on the behinds of those who are not compliant, to providing support for risk-taking that opens up possibilities. Central offices must go from knowing all the answers to creating the questions to be addressed. This is a movement from being the source of information and orders to being the fount of inspiration and possibility. District administrators must move from an attitude of being served to a belief that their role is to serve the needs of school sites. Robert Greenleaf has written eloquently on the idea of servant leadership, and those who should be the best models of that are those who work in the district office. After all, no child learns to read, masters mathematics, or pursues her dreams sitting in a district office. This is done in classrooms. How can district offices serve this process?

There needs to be a movement from operating as channels to creating webs. Channels are linear and direct the flow of things in a certain direction. Yet education is systemic and holistic, and, therefore, it needs the support of a web of strength that will surround and uplift the process.

District staff must move from a preoccupation about things to a focus on process. Counting the state reports or accounting for equipment may be urgent, but it is not important. It is time for district offices to worry about the things that count, rather than counting the things that are worrisome.

Finally, district leaders must begin to focus much of their attention on what is outside the district rather than what is on the inside. The people inside must be empowered to do the work and be protected from outside interference. They must be given the web of support that is available from all the sources that we have thus far kept outside our spheres of influence. District offices must move from keeping their distance to promoting the power of proximity. They have to get close to the customer, and district office customers are the school sites they are supposed to support.

One of the key roles for a superintendent is to create a subversive central office that turns its traditional role and approach upside down so that it supports, and does not hinder, school improvement. What a radical concept!

6

INSPIRATION LIVES ON AFTER THE LEADER IS GONE

Education lost a true hero when Superintendent John Stanford lost his battle with leukemia. Stanford gained national attention when he was named superintendent of the Seattle Public Schools because he was not a traditional educator; he was a retired Army major general. In fact, his success in Seattle has led to a spate of former military officers being named to head school systems.

Equating leadership with former military service misses the point. Stanford was not just a great superintendent because he was a great leader. He was a great leader because he was a great human being. He brought to the position a bone-deep belief in the possibilities of children; an unwavering expectation for excellence from all who worked in, and with, the school system; and an uncanny ability to articulate a message and reach out to the community to bring people in to battle for a better education. He was a charismatic communicator.

When you heard those who knew him talk, they did not mention his medals or ribbons; they talked about his passion for children and how much he cared about them. They did not talk about the way he gave orders and commands; they talked about the way he hugged people, talked to them, and listened. When they talked about John Stanford, they did not talk about the way he could plan an attack on illiteracy; they talked about the way he showed his love. Stanford's motto was "love them and lead them," and he walked his talk.

Stanford was in a hurry. He wanted the best for Seattle's children, and he wanted it now. The only time the major general emerged was when he expressed his high expectations for what he wanted from the children and for the children. He let Seattle know that the whole community was responsible for its children.

He also knew how to delegate. He surrounded himself with those who knew more about education than he did. He understood that a great superintendent is not one who is the source of information. A great superintendent is the source of inspiration.

I first met John at an AASA national conference in Orlando. I was a bit surprised that he was there. After all, he was not a traditional superintendent. Why had he come to our meeting? He quickly let me know. He was there to learn. He told me that he felt like a kid in a candy store. He did not know where to go next. He was having a ball going to sessions and soaking up the knowledge. He could have taken the position that he was a trained leader and had nothing to learn from us. He did the opposite. He expressed his humility over the challenges he faced and acknowledged that he had so much more to learn. That was the moment I became a fan of John Stanford. We all could learn from his openness, his sense of commitment and high expectations, and the strength that he showed through his vulnerability. It has been a sad time for Seattle in losing John. But it gives me hope that people like him can be the kind of superintendents our children deserve.

Another hero of mine is a superintendent in West Des Moines, Iowa. Les Omotani has quietly gone about his work there with none of the fanfare and national attention garnered by John Stanford. However, what Les is doing in West Des Moines is as profound, and perhaps ultimately more far-reaching. Les is trying to operationalize the elements of Stanford's personal style and imbed it in the system.

West Des Moines is trying to make its schools the centers for the community. Omotani, along with his board and staff, is working to make the schools the focal point for community outreach and support for children. By doing so, they are ensuring community support for the school system and for the children. They are also building a stronger community. When superintendents reach out past the traditional boundaries of the school district, they create bonds that make both ends of the chain stronger. This also allows them to strengthen their ability to act and remain as leaders. People value leaders who give value to their lives.

Leadership is not about personal glory or fame. It is not about power and control. It is about taking people where they didn't know they needed to go. It is about taking individuals and teaching them to work together. That is done through communication and compassion. It is carried out through expectation and exhortation, and by perseverance and perspiration. Leadership is about inspiring and conspiring with others to make the community and the children better. It is about loving them and leading them. Keep up the good work, Les. *Vaya con dios,* John.

7

A BALANCE OF
HEAD AND HEART

The superintendency holds an enduring fascination for me. It is a source of pleasure and pain, of peril and promise, of minutiae and mission, of foible and fable.

But what I have been grappling with of late is how little we really understand about the job. I watch great superintendents at work and realize that I am watching artistry. Great superintendents remind me of great athletes who can anticipate where other players will be and who can make a pass that reaches their teammates at just the right moment. The less great superintendents try for the same play and throw it into the stands. What is the difference?

Not only do we not understand the work, but we also lack a good fix on the context of the work. Most studies of the superintendency are quantitative and focus on the numerical issues. What is needed is more understanding gleaned from case studies and ethnographic studies so we can begin to understand this culture known as the superintendency.

AASA hopes to do some of that with foundation support. We also are working with the University Council on Educational Administration on creating a Center for the Superintendency.

A REVEALING MOMENT

Today we need a more basic set of understandings. In a conversation with one of our outstanding superintendents, I got a new insight into the role.

This school leader has a great focus on the work. She sets clear expectations for staff, implements programs aimed at improving student achievement, and has led her school board to new awareness of its role. In general, she does all the things that make her an effective superintendent.

This particular day she was dealing with a child traumatized by the death of her mother in an auto accident. That same day she also had dealt with a violent act in school and counseled a staff member with personal problems.

Each of these issues were matters not of the head but of the heart. I told her she was not just an *effective* superintendent, but she was also an *affective* superintendent. At that moment I learned something new about a profession I have studied for thirty years. You can't do the job focused on only one half of the equation. In educational leadership the headbone has to be connected to the heartbone.

Certainly, school leaders must be effective. That means they have an unwavering commitment to helping the staff and community stay focused. High expectations for all are enforced. Goals must be clear, concise, and pursued with a sense of constancy that lets everyone know there will be no escape.

Further, effective superintendents are communicators of the highest order. They know how to convene and persuade to get everyone aligned to the job at hand. And effective leaders are facilitators. They know how to marshal and organize resources to back up the goals.

But at the risk of being a "bleeding heart," I must say that any school system leader who focuses only on the issues of effectiveness and not on affectiveness is not doing a complete job. Affective leaders have to be about the heart and soul of the organization. They must understand that children who are hungry for food or who are starving for attention will not learn to read until those more basic needs are met.

The affective leader understands that the key to communication is through people's feelings, not through their thoughts. That is why great leaders are storytellers who can use metaphor and fable to help folks anchor their thoughts to their feelings.

Leaders understand that to get folks to perspire, first you have to inspire. And inspiration comes from being grounded in the spirit of the work. That leads to the need for moral courage. Great leaders know what hill they will die on and are clear about which fights must be made.

In this era of accountability, great leaders know that for folks to perform, they first must be given the tools and support. Effective leaders worry about skills and the results they must get. Affective leaders know that the process they use to get there must be grounded in how people feel about the task at hand.

While we don't know nearly enough about the superintendency, we do know that it has to have a head and a heart. And that is a good starting point for any educational experience.

8

A VISION FOR EDUCATION

The alpha of American public schools is Horace Mann. He, more than any other single person, dreamed up the system of common schools that would provide the place where our emerging democracy could find its unity. Economist Lester Thurow reminded us at an AASA National Conference that the most important task facing educators today is to educate all children to be productive citizens. Great men see into the future. Great countries pursue the vision of these great men and make it so.

Horace Mann was a dreamer. He was a visionary. He believed in the American dream and its possibilities. As we move through a new century and millennium, I fear old Horace is tossing and turning in his grave from the nightmare scenario we now face in this country. Horace Mann believed in justice and equity, and in everyone's opportunity to succeed. As we move into the future, I suspect Horace Mann would be horrified at the injustice and inequity our children face.

Our flag salute is a pledge to "liberty and justice for all." It is interesting that those two are paired. You can't have one without the other. And not just for some. They are for all, not just those who live in the right neighborhoods or states or on the right side of the tax break. They are for all. They are for those kids who live in the dark alleys of our nation's conscience. As a nation we have committed to leave no child behind. What are we doing to ensure that noble goal is realized? Once we have tested and disaggregated and committed to end the "soft bigotry of low expectations" that our president frets over, will we have the courage to overcome the hard bigotry of inadequate and unequal resources? Will we have the courage to precede the tests with programs that not only help the kids pass the test but to succeed in life? I would guess these are the kinds of questions Horace Mann would ask.

And what about how we handle our children in school? Horace Mann was skeptical about the role of discipline in school and believed in the need for balance in exercising it. He once said that "the discipline of former times was inexorably stern and severe; even if it were wished, it is impossible to return to it. The preservation of order, together with the proper dispatch of business, requires a mean between the too much and the too little in all evolutions of the school." Horace would have serious questions about the zero tolerance policies of today.

Horace Mann understood that education was a system where all the pieces were linked and could not be uncoupled. He wrote that a "systematic acquisition of a subject knits all parts together, so that they will be longer retained and more easily recalled. To acquire a few of the facts gives us fragments." What would Horace think about our modern system of assessment that tests for "rabbit pellet" chunks of information and ignores that deeper need to think about thinking?

He understood that standards must mean something and that expectations must be interwoven with reality. Again, he said it is not more true in architecture than in education that the value of the work in every upper level depends upon the solidity of all beneath it. The leading prevailing defect in the intellectual department of our schools is the want of thoroughness, a proneness to be satisfied with a verbal memory of rules instead of a comprehension of principles, with a knowledge of the names of things, instead of a knowledge of the things themselves; or if some knowledge of things is gained, it is too apt to be a knowledge of them as isolated facts and unaccompanied by a knowledge of the relations which subsist between them and bind them into a scientific whole.

As we break education into bite-sized chunks and oversimplify learning into that which can be measured, we scramble closer and closer to the edge of the fears expressed by Horace Mann so long ago.

In the current era of zero tolerance, world-class standards, and mechanical fixes, Horace Mann would be sorely out of place as a school reformer—too dreamy, too "touchy feely," too liberal, not hard-nosed enough, and way too soft-hearted. It is my dream that those of us who care about public education and the common schools that were created to carry it out will push against the tide that would wash those goals away in a wave of hard-headed and hard-hearted reforms that are bending the form of public education while losing sight of its substance. We must stand against those who would turn education into a mechanical repair shop in which every child is a cog in the profit-making infrastructure.

We educational leaders are business leaders and we are political leaders. But most importantly, we must be moral leaders, and we must show moral courage in the struggle for our children's future. If we fail, the dreams of Horace Mann will be lost to our children's living nightmare.

9

A NOVEL NOTION

Best Teachers at Poorest Schools

The critics of public education have a million reasons why they think our schools don't work. They cite things like bureaucracy, teacher unions, lack of accountability, and monopolistic practices as reasons why American schools don't keep pace internationally. However, we can't look to the critics for clarity because their concerns are overly simplistic and just plain wrong.

Our schools are much more competitive internationally than the critics admit. How else are we the dominant country in the world? Did all our good things come from private education?

At the basest level, when comparing standardized test scores we hold our own. In most comparisons we end up somewhere in the middle of the pack. Not something to write home about, but no reason for shame. Factoring in all the problems with international comparisons, differences in culture, curriculum, and sampling would minimize any cause for regret.

TOLERATING DISPARITIES

But what is masked in these comparisons is a more basic truth about America's schools that should give us all cause for worry. This truth is that we tolerate great discrepancies in our schools with how we allocate resources to them and how we support them. In fact, a recent international study, when disaggregated, showed American students being among the best and the worst in the world. It just depends on where they go to school.

One of the silver linings in the new accountability push will be the need to disaggregate our data on student achievement. That might lead to a more meaningful discussion on what resources are needed to actually "leave no child behind."

This leads to the other great fallacy that our critics overlook. We really don't have an American educational problem. Our weaknesses are much narrower and more targeted. We have serious problems in schools that enroll a high proportion of low-income children. The reasons are many. They tend to have less social capital (intact homes, families with higher educational attainment, and so on) and less real capital behind them. Schools are funded largely from property taxes, and property taxes tend to be tied to wealth. Wealthy communities raise more money and give it to schools. Poor communities cannot do so.

But the bedrock issue facing schools serving children from low-income families is the quality of their teachers and principals. And that is a variable school districts, states, and the federal government can and must address. The fact is schools with high concentrations of poor children often get the teachers who have been least prepared and who are more likely not to be certified. Those schools also typically have the highest levels of turnover.

How can we expect to improve the learning of students when those leading that learning are the least able to do so? Now let me be clear: There are many fine, dedicated teachers and principals in these schools. But the fact is also clear that there aren't enough, and that there are too many people lacking the training and experience to rise to the challenge.

A paper on this subject developed at AASA by Cindy Prince outlines several key points. First, students most at risk of reading difficulties, poor and minority students, are increasingly isolated in impoverished schools. These schools have fewer resources, greater teacher and administrator shortages, fewer applicants for vacancies, higher absenteeism among teachers, and higher rates of staff turnover.

Much of this turnover is due to the adverse working conditions in these schools. Just as we know that fewer people are entering administration because they do not see the benefits outweighing the costs, we also know that teachers decline to stay long in situations where the benefits don't outweigh the challenges. Placement in difficult assignments without adequate support has been shown to be one of the chief reasons beginning teachers leave the profession. Assigning beginning teachers to low-income schools is not only unfair to the students, but it is also unfair to those teachers and increases the problems that already exist.

A PARTIAL SOLUTION

Most administrators are aware that union contracts frequently control teacher assignment. Superintendents and boards must bear some responsibility for allowing this to happen. But fighting to control teacher assignment is only part of the battle. At some point we must deal with the working conditions in those schools. We need to ensure that our strongest leaders work there and then make it worth their while financially to stay there by giving them the tools they need to succeed. Perhaps classes should be smaller in those schools, more human support offered, and better technology made available.

At some point we need to consider compensation. AASA has suggested an idea that qualified teachers and principals be given federal tax credits for working in struggling schools. This would provide an incentive for recruiting and keeping good people in these schools.

No easy answers or silver-bullet solutions exist to make certain we leave no child behind. But we might start by admitting what the real problems are and then acknowledging that when it comes to poverty, throwing money at the problem is at least a partial solution.

Perhaps we can't keep poor children from being poor, but we can make certain they are given the best teachers and principals possible. It is very American to want to see people pull themselves up by their own bootstraps. First, we must make certain they are wearing boots.

LITERACY LEADERSHIP

From Lynch Mob to Parade

At the beginning of a new year, the party favors are thrown away along with the New Year's resolutions. The wrapping paper is recycled and the tree ornaments banished to storage. It has crossed my mind how much education resembles an overloaded Christmas tree—a big beautiful thing that is cut off from its roots and loaded down with so many glittering objects that its original beauty has been lost.

Every time society has a challenge, education is asked to step in. Consequently, we have been inundated with add-ons to the programs and curriculum until we have become the kings and queens of small ideas. Scratch a school administrator and you will find a thousand ideas for improving schools just under the surface. And we just add them to the tree.

The problem is that small ideas, while useful, don't create a center of gravity or a force powerful enough to change things. That is one reason education has become a place where incremental improvement is the only way. The problem, of course, is that we are living in times where incremental gains aren't enough. What we need is the power of big ideas.

CUTTING EXCUSES

The notion of universal literacy is one of the biggest ideas I have run across. Every child reading. No excuses. Of course, there isn't an educator who will not claim to believe that that is the goal. The problem is, if it is, why are such a large number of our children falling so short of it?

The reasons are many. Many of our schools are grappling with horrendous social conditions that inhibit children's learning. We are torn in a thousand directions by competing mandates. We have more reading programs than we have children to take them. Teachers aren't adequately trained to do the job and so it goes.

The problem, of course, is that these are all excuses. Good excuses, but excuses nonetheless. And we are living in a world where these excuses aren't acceptable because to lack basic literacy skills dooms a child to a lifetime of failure and puts a huge drag on our economic and political systems.

There is no question that literacy is a gateway issue. Without it, the rest of the school day is just time passing. If you can't read, you can't function in school and you can't function outside of school. So if we were to do only one thing, literacy should be it. We have to open that gate wide so that children can pass through it to find their futures.

The good thing about the literacy issue is that while battles have raged over which ways to deliver it—whole language or phonics, for example—virtually no one disagrees that it is important. From the conservative right to the radical left, everyone thinks all children in America deserve to be literate as a basic right. For that reason, literacy is a common ground issue. It is one that can bring people together. To quote President George W. Bush, as far as issues go, "It is a uniter, not a divider." In a world where opposition to ideas is rampant, the smart school administrator should latch onto this one. It will have lots of friends and few enemies.

TOTAL SUCCESS

People are hungering for leadership. Our profession is expected to provide it. Taking the lead on the literacy issue allows the school administrator to get in front of the lynch mob and make it look like a parade. If all school leaders in America made a pledge that they would dedicate themselves to seeing that their schools and school systems focus first and foremost on literacy as the central reason for being and that they would accept nothing short of total success—all children reading by the end of third grade—it would be an act of leadership the likes of which we have not seen in schools.

AASA feels so strongly about this that we have teamed up with an unlikely partner—the Education Commission of the States—to develop a Leadership for Literacy Foundation that will provide support and focus for this issue. We realize state policymakers will have to become a lot smarter about the topic so that policies that move us toward making every child literate are at the forefront of state activity. We also know that local school leaders are going to have to become much better at creating strategic actions to lead local systems toward this goal.

Beyond pledging full leadership to this issue, school leaders will need to act. Meeting this goal will require a series of strategic interventions in what schools do and how they do it. We are going to have to make some really tough decisions on what programs work and get rid of the ones that don't—even if they are sacred cows. We are going to have to make sure that the best teachers are placed with the hardest-to-educate children. We will have to see that principals focus their time and energy on supervising instruction and embedding best practices into their classrooms.

In short, we are going to have to act as instructional leaders—what a concept! This issue will allow us to become what we have always said we were. And that would reconnect us to our roots and clear out our branches so that our children can grow to realize their dreams. Every child reading by third grade. Now there's a New Year's resolution worth keeping.

11

MISSING IN ACTION

The District Office

In the midst of a great era of school reform, something is missing. What is not missing is an emphasis on the bottom and rhetoric from the top.

At the bottom, we have seen an emphasis on the school. The school is where the action is, where the rubber meets the road. Everyone knows that learning takes place in the classroom and if something is going to improve, it must happen there. School reform that starts from the bottom is based on the understanding that those who must change must be involved in the change and those changes must be integrated into the daily work of teachers. It recognizes that education is organic and holistic. Thus we have seen lots of bottom-up reform.

As politicians have become interested, we have witnessed governors, legislators, and state departments of education jumping into the fray. This has ushered in the era of top-down reform, in which coercion and force would create change. This more mechanistic approach relies on external and mechanistic measures to forge improvement.

TOP DOWN AGAIN

Lately there has been a growing awareness that change from the top and change from the bottom are disconnected. Something is missing and that something is the district. From the earliest days of public education in America, districts were created to reflect the desires and will of the community.

They were created to sort out the public's interest in the education of its children. Districts were created for economy and efficiency, but also for embracing communities' values.

For most of our history, districts acted as vehicles of command and control. They were the entity that ensured compliance and outcomes. This was the earliest form of top down, and it didn't work any better at the local level than it is now working at the state level.

Yet there is an important role for districts to play. And for school superintendents to become relevant in the reform movement, this role must be understood and embraced. Actually, there are four reasons for the district to exist: clarity, capacity, coherence, and constancy.

CULTIVATING VISION

Clarity is the "vision thing" that a former president talked about. It is the sense of knowing what ought to be done and what can be gained by connecting to the community, stating that knowledge in ways that everyone understands and then galvanizing action toward it.

The school site is too small a unit for this kind of activity, and the state is much too distant to begin to play the role. Vision that is too close up lacks context, and vision from too great a distance is distorted and faint.

Each district leader must aid the community in understanding its own vision for its children by pulling that vision together and then translating words into actions that the community can rally around. That creates clarity for everyone.

Capacity provides the resources and muscle to get the work done. Site-based reform often flounders because there are just not enough resources at one school to do the job. The loss of economies of scale forces the school to do without needed infrastructure to make it work more effectively. Districts should turn themselves inside out and move from trying to command schools to change to a role of helping them change by serving as the source of needed capacity.

Coherence helps those in schools make sense out of what they are doing by helping create bridges between schools.

One problem with bottom-up reform is that it fails to consider that in our modern, complex society people just don't stay put anymore. They move. And states are much too removed from the lives of people to create the needed connections. Districts offer the perfect resource to help create broader standards for action. This recognizes that no school is an island and that real reform must be connected on a broader scale.

Constancy relates to the reality that change takes time. Change is bigger than a faculty committee or a principal. (It is also bigger than a single superintendent or school board.) Change requires a will to stay the course. Certainly, constancy can come from the state or federal government, although it would appear that these efforts tend to be tied to political expediency rather than a long-term vision. Districts can provide the sense of constancy that allows everyone to understand that what happens this year will be connected to what happened last year and what will happen next year. This allows folks to focus on the task at hand and to understand they can't merely wait things out.

TOUGH TRANSITION

Districts and district leaders have a crucial role in creating better schools. It isn't the role of telling people what they have to do and then enforcing compliant behavior. It isn't merely acting as a cipher for the state to carry out mandates that make no sense. The role is one of creating connected communication and collaborative action that knit the community together, gather its will into action, and bolster these actions by garnering the necessary resources and support.

It is a tough transition from the old role, but in making it, superintendents will become indispensable to the process of change that is swirling around us.

12

TREATING PARENTS
AS OUR CUSTOMERS

We are often told that we should run schools more like businesses. Setting aside the obvious problem that children are not widgets, we still are left with the chore of sorting out who the customers are.

One of the greatest problems of American education is a confusion over who we serve. Some would argue that the children are the customers. They sit in the seat each day receiving instruction. Others believe the community, big business, colleges, or even the military are the customers, since they hire or place the students.

I believe the parent is the customer. Customers are the people who can choose to take their business elsewhere. Students are captive to the process, and the broader community must live with the product regardless. Students should be considered the workers, since it is their productivity that really counts. The broader community, business, and the rest are the shareholders. They own stock in the operation. These distinctions become very important when you understand that shareholders have very different expectations and values than customers. Shareholders want return on investment. Customers want value and service.

PARENTAL SAVVY

With this in mind, AASA conducted a major poll of public school parents—our customers. And what we found out was fascinating.

We found that parents really get it. They have a very sophisticated understanding of their children's schools and what their children need.

Far too often, educators, policymakers, and critics have underestimated parents and their knowledge of what makes a good school or how good their own children's schools are. Our study showed us we underestimate them at our own peril. Parents can be and should be the school system leader's greatest ally. They want what is best for their children—so should you.

Our study gives us much to celebrate and some things to be concerned about. It provides a clear set of issues for the savvy school leader.

First, the good news. Parents of public school children generally are very pleased with their children's education. They feel, overall, that schools are doing pretty well. They see some things we could be doing better, but the general mood is positive and upbeat. They like the idea of public school choice, but a majority believe they already have choice and don't see choice as something that would lead to big improvements in their schools.

That tells us that years of rhetoric and millions of dollars have not created as much traction on the voucher issue as proponents would have liked. In fact, three out of four never have considered pulling their children out of public schools. They are very supportive of the values that underpin public education and see public schools as the place where common American values are taught and caught. However, that also tells us that one in four has had concerns and should cause us to wonder what we should be doing better.

The study offers clues. For example, the biggest issue for parents is student safety, and they feel that disruptive students should be excluded from regular classrooms. But they also want to see that these students receive an education in alternative programs. They understand that learning cannot happen in an environment that is unsafe or disrupted. But they also understand that a society that tosses its problems on the street is a society that will pay a much higher price later on.

Parents want to have meaningful involvement in their children's education. And to the extent that they feel involved, they are more positive.

One way of making this happen is to provide parent centers and academies in schools. Parents who feel a strong sense of influence over their children's education are the ones least likely to have thoughts of removing their children from public schools or supporting vouchers.

GOOD BUSINESS FOR ALL

While parents understand what many policymakers have not grasped—that tests are useful tools for assessing how well things are going—they don't think tests are the goal. The most important thing for them is to see their children excited about learning. They know that life is much more than a test, and they don't want to see the curriculum narrowed only to prepare kids for tests. They think we are doing exactly that.

The highest value for parents is to have children who are safe and who are excited about their learning. If that happens they believe the tests will take care of themselves.

Despite the negative publicity schools get, good news resonates more powerfully with parents than does bad news. And the most trusted source of information for them is their own child.

Any good public relations program must start with the children. A good start would involve teachers asking children every afternoon to recap what they did in school today and then to ask them what they did that was most exciting. Children who can go home excited about what they did in school are worth more than gold.

Parents want smaller classes, particularly in the lower grades, good teachers in their classrooms who light their children's fires, good principals who involve parents in the learning enterprise, and up-to-date textbooks.

Superintendents who can design systems to produce these things have job security for life. And that would be good business for everyone.

Part II

PUTTING KIDS FIRST

I have found the recent emphasis on running schools like businesses to be curious. Don't get me wrong. When you have hundreds or thousands of employees, budgets with lots of zeros after the first numbers, fleets of buses, and millions of dollars worth of land and buildings, you had best have some sound business practices to fall back on. But the center of the business of education is first and foremost the children; that is what makes it different, interesting, and an awesome responsibility. Public schools are the court of last resort for children. Even private schools aren't so much about children as they are about familial expectations. For, if private schools didn't exist, there would still be a place for the children—public schools. If public schools ceased to exist, where would the tired, the poor, the huddled masses go for their education?

The other thing that gets lost in the rhetoric of school reform is that for many children, school is the place where many of their noneducational needs are met. For many it is the place where they find a warm heart and a hot meal. It is where their eyes are checked and their hearts are mended. Children make the job of educational leader a calling. And our obligation as leaders is to see that other people's children have the same chance at the brass ring as we would want for our own children. We have meaning in our lives by giving the children we serve a chance in theirs.

13

IT TAKES A VILLAGE TO RAISE ACHIEVEMENT

I realize the longer I live in Washington, D.C., the less difference I see between the political parties. What appear to be great gulfs to most of America are small creeks inside the Beltway. There are several reasons for this.

First, differences are exaggerated because folks want to create a reason for people to vote for their party or candidate and against their opposition. Second, no one really has the answers to the tough problems facing America. If they did, those problems would have been solved, so instead people exaggerate small answers into big-time solutions.

Finally, most of the answers available are pretty much in the center of the political spectrum and, therefore, open season for everyone to claim.

SIMILAR MOTTOES

Education is one of those mainstream topics. Watching the current administration and the last one in action makes the point. To date, I see few differences. Sure, there is the issue of vouchers here and class size there, but the basic policy pronouncements are similar. More accountability and more testing.

The former first lady adopted the proverb, "It takes a village to raise a child." The current White House wants to "leave no child behind." The irony of this administration's motto is that it has been the motto of Marion Wright

Edelman and the Children's Defense Fund for years—an organization for which Hillary Clinton served as legal counsel and as a board member.

The reality is that the current administration is right—no child should be left behind. For that to become reality, more than calls for accountability and testing in schools will be required. The last administration was also right—the village will have to be brought into the fray.

One of the most insightful writers on education today is Richard Rothstein, who serves as a research associate for the Economic Policy Institute and as a weekly columnist for the *New York Times*. In a study he conducted in 2000, Rothstein turned the voucher argument upside down. He pointed out that middle-class parents always have had the power to choose which school their children would attend—an argument used by voucher proponents. Rothstein says that the real solution is to give poor people the power to choose where to live. And that's where the village argument comes to the front.

The reality is that the quality of schools has been and continues to be tied very tightly to the level of wealth or poverty of the children the school serves. The greatest variable for SAT scores has been family income. The secret for raising SAT scores is to get children born into wealthier families—or to enroll them in schools where lots of other kids had that advantage. This is not an issue of genetics; it is an issue of advantage and available social capital.

Rothstein argues that families, communities, peer groups, culture, economic markets, and schools are all educational institutions. Changes in any of these can affect student performance. The report written by Rothstein called "Improving Educational Achievement" argues that "most analyses today conclude that 75 percent of the variation in student achievement is attributable to student social and economic characteristics. . . . An assumption that schools are the primary institutional influence, with others acting only as school modifiers, is without theoretical basis."

POVERTY AND PRIVILEGE

No one is arguing that schools don't have a role and that more resources will not help. But it should be clear to anyone that to make a difference in the lives of children, more than a focus on schools will be required. The current administration's discussion on strengthening Head Start is the kind of worthy first step that must be considered.

No one is arguing that responsible assessment should not be a part of an educational improvement strategy. And holding schools and others accountable for their part of the solution is sound both intellectually and morally. Schools that fail children or that discriminate against children should be radically altered.

Schools must focus on knowing which children are being left behind. That means the assessments we have must be disaggregated by race and social class so we know who is being underserved. Schools also must work hard to connect learning to students in meaningful and engaging ways. And interventions must be made to alter the trajectory of students' lives when we find they are not on a successful path. Summer school, after school, and intensive tutorial programs must be tried. And we have to use the research on what works.

But if we are to truly be a nation where the children of poverty are able to run alongside the children of privilege, then a total strategy and a commitment by all is needed. The village must be galvanized to action. Merely letting some children escape a school that has failed to overcome the 75 percent of non-school issues doesn't seem to be a sound strategy. Engaging the village in a rededication to other people's children might be a better way.

MAKING KIDS
STRONGER BY MAKING
THEM FLEXIBLE

It has always interested me why some people bend while others break.

I suppose I am interested because, like many others, my own story is one of resilience. My academic career marked my movement from being a non-reader to slow learner to underachiever to honor student. I always have credited my progress to the support of parents and teachers and to an incredibly strong streak of stubbornness that has served me well.

The exercise of will throughout my life has allowed me to forge through the unknown, to stand strong in the winds of change, and to exhibit a sense of self-worth even when external circumstances would question my self-confidence.

Yet human will, by itself, can merely be aggravating to others or even self-destructive. It has to be balanced by flexibility. I call this paradox *confident humility*.

A POST-COLUMBINE WORRY

Confident humility is the ability to believe in yourself while leaving room for the possibility that someone else has a better idea. I think the sense of balance implied by this paradox is a key to unlocking our understanding of resiliency. The healthiest place is between the extremes. If you lean too far in one direction, it's easy to be pushed over. A sense of balance allows you to recover and to adjust.

How can schools build the strong, healthy ego implied by that sense of balance? In the wake of Columbine, that question becomes even more pertinent and powerful. How can we help our children grow up, unscarred and unscathed, in a changing and disconnected world where images of violence permeate? How can we give children a sense of purpose, a sense of confidence and a sense of balance when everything around them seems to question purpose, destroy confidence, and knock them down before they even get started?

The power of teaching resilience is the power of giving children the strength to handle change and to recover easily from misfortune. Sadly, for many of our children, misfortune is a way of life. How can we, as adults, prepare students for what they need to be resilient people?

Hillary Rodham Clinton wrote a book a few years ago and took the title from the African proverb that states, "It takes a village to raise a child." This proverb recognizes the creation of resilient children is not something done only in a home or in isolation. It requires a team. Unfortunately, in today's world we must ask: If it takes a village to raise a child, what does it take to raise a village?

Far too many of our children are growing up in a world where there is no village—no safety net of support to catch them when they fall. They are growing up isolated and emotionally neglected. Their emotional care and feeding is being left up to the schools. And far too often, the schools are not up to it. They cannot be parent, friend, mentor, guide, doctor, nurse, social worker, and minister. The task is too overwhelming. It does take the village.

RISK-TAKING FACTORS

That is why a national movement is needed to bind school, family, and community together. The movement toward "schools of promise," which grew out of the America's Promise initiative led by Gen. Colin Powell, is one way of connecting schools to communities. The initiative is rooted in the reality that schools exist at the physical and psychological centers of what can become the village. By helping schools reach out to the community and the community to reach in to the schools, we can begin building villages around our children.

This effort must be done with a sense of respect and mutuality. There is another proverb less well known but just as appropriate. It reminds us that "when elephants fight, the grass gets trampled." When adults fight, children suffer. Resilience in children starts with adults acting responsibly and respectfully toward each other. Resilience doesn't just happen. It is created by caring adults. If we expect children to show respect, they must be shown respect and witness it in the adults they observe.

Researchers at the University of Minnesota established that a strong connection to school reduces the risk-taking behaviors that lead to failure. School connection also enhances those behaviors that lead to success. This provides clues to what we must do to create resilient young people. We must find ways to get them connected to school. Caring adults must create a web of support around children for them to grow with a sense of efficacy, which becomes the foundation for resilient behavior. Schools are there to elevate a child's chances for success.

UNCERTAIN TIMES

Rubber bands are resilient. But their resilience is more than just snapping back into place once they are pulled. They store and release kinetic energy. As any teacher knows, rubber bands are good at propelling small objects. If we are to give our children the gift of success, we must find ways of helping them prosper in an uncertain and, too often, unfriendly environment.

We want children to snap back, to recover, and to adjust. We also want them to move forward, to propel themselves with the confident humility that will lead to their success. Through their success, we want them to blaze a trail for all of us.

15

BEING MINDFUL WHAT YOU WISH FOR

Have you ever thought about the fact that zero-tolerance policies, high-stakes assessment, and the ending of social promotion are all branches from the same tree? All three premises have their roots in the idea that the best way to develop children is by destroying them.

Now that statement seems harsh, but the fact is that when a child is removed from school, his future is destroyed. When he is held back to repeat a grade, his future is imperiled. So why are we doing this?

Two reasons leap to mind. The first is that politicians have required it. But the second is that we school leaders wish to look decisive and unafraid of setting high standards. Let me remind you that we need to be careful of what we wish for because we might get it.

PLENTY OF ATTENTION

We wished that people would pay more attention to education. We got *A Nation at Risk* and dozens of studies that followed. Sadly, their sole purpose seemed to be to demonstrate to the public how badly we were performing. We hoped politicians would pay more attention to education so that we would get more resources. We got the president's summit and the national goals. I'm still waiting for them to show me the money. We wanted the public to believe we could take their concerns seriously, so we jumped on the standards and accountability bandwagon and rode along. If we are not careful, that bandwagon is headed for the ditch.

Today it is difficult for a school leader to oppose standards and accountability. These watchwords are the apple pie and motherhood of education. If you oppose them, you are painted as a "contrarian" or an "apologist" who doesn't want to change or improve. It seems good politics to get ahead of the mob and make it look like a parade. And even though zero-tolerance policies and high-stakes assessment were created by politicians outside the educational community, school leaders are pushing for higher test scores, tougher discipline codes, and greater accountability. Many now have incentives built into their contracts for increases in student performance.

Please consider these practices a warning sign. Our eagerness to go along and get along with those who are pushing these movements will rebound back on our heads. When these efforts fail, scapegoats will be sought and educators will take the fall for it, not those who created the movement.

WAYWARD ASSUMPTIONS

The assumption driving the high-stakes testing movement is that for America to be competitive we must raise our standards. Aren't we already the dominant country in the world? Certainly we know many of our children are not achieving the American dream and to the extent that our expectations are too low for them, we should raise them and demand better.

But we must recognize that in many cases success will require more resources. A multiple-choice test isn't enough. Just as NASA may have to rethink its policy of "faster, cheaper, better" in the wake of some recent failures, we must understand that just because norm-referenced tests are faster and cheaper, they may not be better than providing the support needed to prepare children for better performance.

The assumption driving the zero-tolerance movement is that schools need to be safer and that the way to make them safe is to get rid of the troublemakers. We do need to make schools safer. The problem is that zero tolerance is also zero judgment. Not every kid who breaks a rule is a troublemaker. Not every rule that is broken should be treated in the same way. We have no problem seeing the inherent unfairness in mandatory sentences for prisoners. Isn't a zero-tolerance policy fraught with the same narrow vision? As the results of these policies pile up in schools, as we see the children who fail the tests being retained in grade and dropping out, and as we witness the human tragedy that entails, we need to remember where the blame will be placed. As we see children excluded from school for momentary lapses of judgment or for violating rules in a silly way (the expulsion of students for bringing Midol or a fingernail file to school leap to mind), we must remember who will be blamed for doing these stupid things. It will not be the politicians who passed the zero-tolerance laws or the legislatures that created statewide testing systems. It will be the local school administrators who are implementing the policies.

When we take on the role of school leaders, we inherit the responsibility for acting as leaders. Leaders don't blindly follow silly mandates or rules without questioning them. They don't embrace laws that relieve them of acting responsibly on behalf of children. And leaders don't jump on bandwagons so they can keep their jobs. Leaders get in front of the wagon to make sure it stays on the road. If we don't do that, we can rest assured we will get zeroed out when someone turns on the fan.

16

SET THE RECORD STRAIGHT

Put Children First

The beginning of school is a good time to reflect on the changes we would like to make, or see made, in our work. To a great extent, we have the power and ability to shape our own destiny. As educational leaders, we have a responsibility to take charge of our own destinies. We must move from seeing ourselves as victims and having a sense of hopelessness and helplessness to positioning ourselves as victors.

It is important that we recognize the way things should be. By doing so, we might find a way to make it so. With that in mind, let me provide a modest list as a starting point:

Focus on the real problems and set straight those whose perceptions are based upon myth or distortion.

So much of what the public thinks about education is based upon what our critics have chosen to tell them and the way the press has chosen to report that information. Much of what the public thinks is wrong. The public knows that today's schools are not as good as they once were and that they have deteriorated. They know that educators are not motivated to change, that schools are unsafe, and kids are shiftless. They know this because it is what they have been told.

In my travel, I spend a lot of time on airplanes. I get the opportunity to talk to businesspeople who are convinced that schools in this country do not measure up to those in other countries, and that the quality of education is not as good as it was when they went to school. By the end of the ride, through providing a few facts and some perspective, I have gotten them to realize that the way they have looked at education has been distorted by what they have been told and that there is much more to the story. Each of us should make it our mission to set the record straight.

Affirm, rather than attempt to bludgeon educators to greatness.

It is amazing to me that otherwise intelligent people resort to a form of psychic corporal punishment as a means to encourage improvement. Yes, the stick can get the horse to move, but the carrot leads it to the right destination.

It is difficult to achieve peak performance when you have had your soul robbed of hope. How many of us turn around and do the same thing to those who work with us and for us? There is a sign that you sometimes see in offices that reads, "The beatings will continue until morale improves." The humor of the sign comes from the irony that morale will never improve while the beatings continue.

Likewise, schools will not improve as long as we rely on external, negative reinforcement to inspire people to excellence. We must build on what is good if we hope to get better.

Lead, and get involved in school reform.

Today we have reform that seems to be based on an "educator-proof" model. Business and political leaders get together, without educators present, to discuss how to improve education. Think tanks, foundations, and various gurus expound on what should be done without involving educators in their discussions. We have "nontraditional leaders" and "alternative certification" to ensure that education is not left in the hands of the educators, and systemic reform that does not address school systems, which are the only systems we have.

When all the shouting is done, and when everyone has come down from the various summits being held, the classroom teachers, principals, and superintendents will be the only ones left to clean up and move forward. We can start by taking on the challenge. We, who are being overlooked, must take responsibility for proving that we know what we are doing. Then we must do it.

Keep the classroom in the crosshairs of school reform.

Federal tests, standards, advanced certification, vouchers or charters, site-based management, or block scheduling: Many of these ideas have merit and may be worth doing. But they all hinge on a central question: Will they get past the classroom door?

If you want to make education better, you have to start in the classroom. As system leaders, that must be our mantra and our focus. Everything else is hype. Reform must be centered on the relationship between teacher and child.

Put children first.

There is an African proverb that says that when the elephants fight, the grass gets trampled. I once had a sign that read, "The time for action is past, now is the time for senseless bickering." I put it away because so many people were already acting on that sentiment. The sad fact is that when adults bicker, the children suffer. Most school systems exist as places for adult employment and adult political play. Review the time you spend in cabinet or board meetings on adult issues, as opposed to the time you spend asking what is best for children and addressing issues that directly affect them. Unless children are at the center of what we do, what we do has no center.

17

CANDLES IN
THE WIND

Although Princeton and Washington Heights are only forty miles apart, they are two different worlds in terms of the lives that children in those two places lead.

One year, shortly before Christmas, I attended my daughter's midwinter concert, held in the chapel of Princeton University. The Gothic cathedral, with its stained glass windows, vaulted ceiling, and cavernous acoustics, is an inspiring setting for such an event. The students of Princeton High are lucky to have such a place for their concert.

The robed choir entered from the rear, marching down the center aisle, between the rows of well-dressed parents, each member holding a flickering candle while singing a work by one of the great classical composers. The entire concert consisted of one classical piece after another, sung in the original language of German, French, or Italian. The concert ended with Handel's *Hallelujah Chorus*, a celebration of birth and possibility.

These children have had the best of what money can buy. In our society, a great childhood leads to the possibility of a successful adulthood. My daughter and her classmates were on their way to a march through life with the pomp and circumstance that advantage can offer.

The next evening I traveled a short distance up the turnpike to visit with a friend who was a middle school principal in a predominantly Dominican section of New York. There was a ceremony at her school, but its focus was on death, not birth.

It took place on the asphalt surface of the playground, where hundreds had gathered to mourn the deaths of three young men who had been killed in a car accident. The mourners were huddled in the chilly night air shivering in their logo jackets and knit caps. The young men had been gang members that the principal had found on the street. She had created a program for them so they could finish high school. Every day after the younger children left, these young men came in to study for their GED. Like the kids in Princeton, these young immigrants had dreams. The opportunity to pursue those dreams had been rekindled in them, only to be snuffed out in a senseless accident.

The service started with the lighting of candles from a flame that was passed among the mourners, illuminating the sad faces as the flame passed by. As the candles flickered in the cold December evening, those who had gathered remembered their friends with laughter, tears, and songs sung in their native language, Spanish. These young men had come to America to find something better. Instead they had found gangs, poverty, and death that came too soon.

Still, they believed in America. In the middle of the service, a long white limousine slid by. Several young men popped out of the sunroof, shouting and cheering. These were members of another gang, celebrating the deaths of their rivals. What kind of world have we given our children that some would celebrate the deaths of others? Why did they feel that they could succeed only if their rivals failed? In the land of plenty, isn't there enough to go around?

I looked up above the school and spied the American flag, lit by one spotlight, snapping sharply in the brisk night air. It is the same flag that flies over Princeton and all the other places of privilege in our country. It is the same flag that flies over Harlem and Scarsdale and Davis Creek, West Virginia, where I grew up. Although Princeton and Washington Heights are only forty miles apart, they are two different worlds in terms of the lives that children in those two places lead. The same is true for all the have and have-not communities in our nation.

Yet, all of these children are a part of America—a country whose flag we ask them to salute and to offer their pledge that we are one nation, under God, indivisible, with liberty and justice for all.

I reminded myself that on this earth, God's work must be our own. If we are to be indivisible, we must see that there is liberty and justice for everyone, not only those who live in the right communities, with the best of possibilities. If we as a nation are to really give the children of Washington Heights the same opportunities afforded those in Princeton, we must dedicate our lives to keeping the flames of their candles burning brightly, so that nights of mourning can turn into mornings of celebration, and so that the spirit of the *Hallelujah Chorus* can resound for all our children, not only the privileged few.

18

REJOICING IN A COMMUNITY WITH HIGH EXPECTATIONS

Shortly before Christmas I went back to Princeton to see my daughter perform in the annual winter concert that the high school presents in the university chapel. It is an event that has taken place for more than fifty years and has outlived numerous principals, superintendents, countless school board members, and has even weathered several church-state controversies. The mood is reverent and the event is an annual highlight for the community.

As I sat listening to what is arguably the finest high school choir in America (I know I'll get letters from some of you begging to differ, but it really is a very remarkable program), I found myself thinking about our current reform agenda and what it has to do with the program I was witnessing. I came up with nothing. In fact, it would probably undermine the excellence I was witnessing. What I was seeing and hearing was so far beyond the so-called world-class standards that are being ballyhooed that there is no comparison. All of our children should have the opportunity that the children of Princeton have. To make this a reality, we should see what in Princeton should be replicated.

Again, I am going to get letters chastising me for having the audacity to suggest that what is provided in an exclusive, and somewhat idyllic, suburb is replicable across our diverse and inequitable country. Yet are we not wasting our time talking about setting standards that will bring all of our children up to world-class levels if it is not replicable? What we want for our own children is what we should want for all children. Why shouldn't the standard be the best of what we have to offer, rather than what is the most ordinary?

I find it remarkable that we can have many discussions about school improvement in this country without ever talking about resources. The standards movement received a death blow at its very inception when "opportunity to learn" standards were eliminated. Setting outcomes without providing the means to get to them is educational insanity. What, then, can we glean from a Princeton choir experience? First and foremost, the community has consistently provided the resources needed to get the job done. The community pays high taxes so that the schools are well funded. The program starts in kindergarten, with each school having a full-time music teacher, and continues with an eight-period day in high school so students can study arts and academics.

There also has been a constancy of purpose. As school boards changed, as superintendents came and went, as principals turned over, it was always clear that Princeton had a world-class music program. It was up to the policymakers and those who implemented those policies to see that the program was protected and advanced.

The first Princeton concert I attended was in 1977, my first year as superintendent. My board strongly suggested that I attend. They were right. I was stunned by the quality of the program, and I received the enlightenment that they had hoped I would. The music program was a cornerstone for the system and in many ways a metaphor for the community's expectations; I would be well served to support it. I got the message.

There also has been emphasis on outstanding instruction. During the last fifty years, there have been only a few choral directors at Princeton, and each has been outstanding. On those rare occasions when they had to replace the director, the district spared no expense or effort to seek the best in the country. All vacancies should be filled with that kind of care and attention.

The director who was there during my tenure, Bill Tregoe, was one of the best teachers I have ever seen. It was not only his sense of music, but his ability to inspire each of the students to give the best they had that I found so tremendous. Great teachers reach down inside students to find what they themselves do not know is there, and pull it out of them. The root word of *education* is *educare*, to bring forth. Great teachers do not invoke, they evoke.

The parents of these children are greatly supportive of the process. That is evident in their attendance at performances, through their significant fund-raising which allows the group to go to Europe every few years, and in their total commitment to backing the school and the directors in their work.

Finally, the biggest lesson from the concert is what the kids contribute. They bring everything they have. They know that everyone has high expectations, that this is a public performance where they will display what they can do, and that they will have to perform at a peak level. They also know that choir members from the past will be there to see if the new group is holding up the tradition. The pressure is on, but it has been internalized—they want to do well.

As we talk about standards, I wish we would talk more about expectations, because that is really what is needed. We need to have very high expectations for our kids and help them internalize those expectations. At the end of the concert, the choir alumni are invited to come forward and join in singing Handel's *Hallelujah Chorus*. If we could help all of our schools find the sense of tradition in excellence that I witnessed on that chilly December evening, it would be a time for all of us to rejoice.

Part III

THE VALUE OF PUBLIC EDUCATION

I have told people that whatever I have achieved in life was not in spite of public schools, it was because of them. It was in the public school classroom of Mrs. Spurlock at Davis Creek Elementary School in Davis Creek, West Virginia, where she suggested that I learned to read and by doing so found a wide world and a mysterious universe was waiting to be explored. It was in the public school classroom of Mrs. Crum in Barboursville, West Virginia, that she suggested to me that perhaps I should think about writing. It was in the public school classrooms in Milton, West Virginia, that Mr. Ball suggested that success in life was in my hands and where Mrs. Sang made me believe I was college material. Later, it was in the ivy-covered and privileged halls of Harvard University where I learned that what I had been given in those threadbare classrooms in West Virginia had grounded me in the values and instilled in me the confidence to compete with the best.

It is my firm and passionate belief that public schools have been given a bum rap. It is in the public school classrooms of America that political and business leaders have been nourished, military leaders have been given their values of service, and the bulk of this nation has been given its generosity of spirit and its common vision of what America could become.

Do public schools have problems? You bet they do. Too many classrooms are still too segregated, too boring, and too inequitable. Too many classrooms challenge too little and chastise too much. Not every school is safe, although we now know that school is the safest place a child is likely to be. There is, indeed, much to be done. But it seems to me silly and, in fact, quite dangerous to our society to undermine and weaken the one institution that has been the engine of our common dreams.

So I will continue to stand up for public schools, even as I point out how they can do better. It is all right to criticize that which we love as long as we do so in a loving manner. I challenge the supporters of public schools to work for their improvement. But I also challenge those who are working to undermine public schools to provide a plausible vision for how a country of civic virtue for all can be created without them.

19

CONFRONTING THE PRESENT WITH HONESTY

When I lived in the desert, there were sometimes tremendous electrical storms. One night I was in bed during one of these storms and every time there was a crash of thunder, I pulled the covers over my head. Then I realized that while thunder makes the noise, lightning does the killing. I was responding to the wrong stimulus.

We in American education have become reactionaries. We respond to the noises around us and ignore the real dangers that are far too often silent. Our critics have made much over the deterioration of public education. In fact, it has become a cottage industry. We are not as good as we once were. School people are lazy and uncaring. Test scores are down or stagnant. Schools are not safe. The only solution is competition or high-stakes tests or doing away with social promotion or bringing in the generals to straighten out the mess. I have called this the case of "drive-by critics and silver-bullet solutions."

BETTER THAN EVER

The fact is that schools are better than ever at carrying out their traditional mission. More kids today are completing high school and going on to college than ever before. Test scores actually are a positive story because they have been renormed upward several times in the last few decades, and children who take the tests are younger than previous generations.

Because we have a broader slice of our population aspiring to attend college, we have a wider cross-section taking the entrance exams. We also face an increasingly diverse student body, many more of whom do not use English as a first language. This tends to suppress reading scores. We must cope with more children coming from homes where poverty robs them of their futures. International comparisons, while interesting, are largely specious, as cultures, curriculums, and samples are so varied that comparisons are meaningless.

Yes, we are, in fact, doing better at our traditional mission, but the whole discussion is meaningless. Our mission is outdated and our progress is insufficient to deal with a changing environment. We have made incremental progress in an exponential environment. We are gradually getting better, while the deteriorating condition of children and the escalating demands of the workplace exceed our capacity to respond. We could well spend the next few years using our time and energy to reform our schools and find that in a few years we are better than we are today and further behind.

We must forget about reforming or restructuring our schools and focus on fundamentally transforming them. We will need to do so, not because we have failed, but because the river of life has continued to flow and we must go with it.

Beyond the need for real transformation lies the quiet lightning that we do not discuss or acknowledge—the dual strands of our societal genetic undoing: race and poverty. These are the challenges that, if left unmet, eventually will be the undoing of our great experiment in democracy.

POWER OF DREAMS

The real power of America always has been in its dreams. No matter where you come from, you always have a chance of going somewhere better. Imagine for a moment a world where that is not true. You are caught, helpless in the social undertow of a society in which your color or your accent or your parents' station determines your own future. How would you feel? What frustration or hopelessness or rage would that create for you?

We know already that the quality of our schools is largely determined by the concentration of poverty in those schools. We know that the most telling variable in test results is family income. We know that despite cries to the contrary, we as a country still tend to look at external differences far more than we should, and ignore internal similarities far more than we ought.

I believe that many of those calling for vouchers and charters quite simply want their children to be able to attend school with other children who look and think like they do. A recent study by the Public Agenda Foundation merely confirmed this thought. Race trumps idealism and social class trumps race. People do not mind their children going to school with children of another race, so long as they share the same values and expectations. Those tend to be shaped by the social class from which they come. Sadly, in America, a large overlap still exists between race and social class.

Yet we do not talk much about it. Again, the Public Agenda Foundation found that white America does not like to discuss race, and when it does, it does so very carefully. However, if we do not face the dangers, we are apt to succumb to them. Perhaps we can move toward the future with more confidence if we are willing to face the present with more honesty. It is time to sort the thunder from the lightning.

PRESERVING PUBLIC EDUCATION, NOT PUBLIC SCHOOLS

Public education is in a period of extreme danger. The threat comes not only from the critics and from those who would destroy public education through vouchers or other means. It comes from a dramatically changing world that allows students and parents to access learning without going to a formal institution called school.

In the words of technology guru Donald Tapscott, we have been "disintermediated," much as the church was after the invention of the printing press.

This dual threat—from those who would dismantle us in the name of improvement and from the simple reality of emerging alternative channels to learning—ultimately endangers not only public schools but our democracy as well. We cannot hope to remain America if we lose the values that have underpinned our democracy and that have been transferred through public education.

HEART AND SOUL

However, we must guard against a blind adherence to old ways of doing business. What must be preserved is public education, not public schools. Public education is the substance. Public schools are merely the form. We must remain open to other forms of delivering the substance. That calls for us to be open and creative. School system leaders must not stand in the schoolhouse door in an effort to block any idea or innovation that might threaten our old forms. We must continue to act as the heart and soul of the values that were once embedded in these old forms.

My father, who was a minister, used to tell me that his job was to comfort the afflicted and afflict the comforted. I think this is the proper role of any leader. Therefore, we must continue to play our key dual role of helping our communities understand that our schools are better than they think and our staffs to understand they are not as good as they need to be. We have to be courageous champions, standing up for the needs of children. We have to be the community conscience, reminding the adults of their obligations to everyone's children, not only their own. We have to be battlers for equity, seeing to it that the playing field is a level one where all have a chance to reach the American dream.

We also have to be collaborative catalysts who find ways to blend the talents and powers of everyone toward a common end. There is much concern over the privatization of public schools and vouchers. We must continue to work against a system that would divide the "haves" from the "have-nots." However, I believe we can expect parts of the educational process to be privatized and our role is to act as brokers, ensuring that the quality of service is of the highest level and that all children benefit. This also should lead to finding ways of weaving the community together into a supportive web for all children.

A SYSTEMIC ORGANISM

School systems exist in the intersections of most communities. We are centered psychically and geographically in the center of things and we have the opportunity to help build villages around children. If it takes a village to raise a child, it takes real leadership to raise a village. Our modern world has burned the villages of our past and we must work to rebuild the sense of common good that once existed.

Finally, we must fight to help people understand that the interconnected nature of things is vital for success. While top-down reform has its place and bottom-up reform has its merits, something must connect the two, and that something is the system. Education is a living, breathing organism that cannot be taken apart or fixed in pieces, as one might fix a mechanical apparatus. It is organic and must be improved systematically. The role of school systems and school system leaders is to attend to all the parts.

Common schools are not vital to the future of America, but the notion of common values and common understandings are. We must fight against the idea of standing up for the status quo, but we must see to it that the core values of inclusiveness, fairness, and equity are preserved in whatever emerges from the current struggles. We must have the courage and the heart to provide the kind of leadership to our institutions and our communities that will allow all of our children to have a chance at the American dream.

21

SUPERINTENDENTS

Stewards of the Good Society

One of the greatest challenges to school leaders is having enough time to read and replenish the well of ideas that each of us needs in order to provide nourishment to those we lead. One of the things I have tried to do for you from time to time is to point you toward some books that might stimulate your thinking. I read one such book, *The Good Society*, by John Kenneth Galbraith. In this book, Galbraith, an economist, attempts to lay out the elements of what makes up a good society.

The good society is one in which every member, regardless of race, gender, or ethnic origin, should have access to a rewarding life. Essentially, a good society is the one our forefathers intended when this country was built. Since education, by its very essence, is about that task, I was drawn to the book.

Galbraith points out the United States has evolved away from a good society. He points to the discrepancy between funding for public and private activities. Private activities tend to be well funded and first-rate. Public activities tend to be less funded and meet lower standards. Housing in parts of some cities is elegant, while the streets and sidewalks that bind them are filthy. Children attend underfunded and chaotic schools and then go home and watch expensively produced television programs.

While the bulk of Galbraith's analysis is economic, a centerpiece of the book concerns itself with what he considers to be the decisive role of education. First, he points out that the good society cannot accept that education in the modern economy is primarily to service economic ends. Education also has a bearing on social peace and tranquility. He states, "Education provides hope and the reality of escape from the lower and less-favored social and economic strata to those above. . . . Perhaps the best in education should be for those in the worst of social situations. They are the most in need of the means for escape."

In the good society, though, there are two other purposes for education. One is to allow people to govern themselves intelligently and the other is to allow them to enjoy life to its fullest.

In reading Galbraith, it struck me that in our instrumentally based approach to education, driven by big business and the demands of the marketplace, we have really lost sight of the broader ends of education.

We have to remember that education not only makes democracy possible, education makes democracy necessary. People need to remember the public tasks, but education also reminds them that they must be seen and heard if these tasks are to be accomplished.

If you want compliant and quiet people, then leave them uneducated. Education tends to lead to a certain outspokenness—something that has been a mark of American culture and may well stem, in part, from our emphasis on universal education. As we march toward a two-tiered system of education, which is inevitable if the proponents of vouchers get their way, we have to wonder what will happen to our democracy. The fact is that education is "most of all, for the enlargement and the enjoyment of life," as Galbraith points out, and if we do not give those most in need the best of education, "we have perhaps the most brutal form of social discrimination: some, as a matter of course, are awarded the full enjoyments of life; many are not."

Finally, Galbraith reminds us of something you must share with your communities: "There is no test of a good society so clear, so decisive, as its willingness to tax—to forgo private income, expenditure and the expensively cultivated superfluities of private consumption—in order to develop and sustain a strong educational system for all its citizens." By that measure, we have a ways to go in America before we are a good society. Part of our mission as leaders is to remind ourselves and those around us of the possibilities and imperatives we share. We are, in essence, stewards for the good society.

22

NO REASON FOR SHEEPISHNESS ABOUT OUR SCHOOLS

As a defender of public education, I often run into people who are very concerned that I am saying good things about public education. They feel it needs great improvement and that I am encouraging apathy.

I guess the idea here is if you can't say something bad about public education, don't say anything at all. It also assumes that those working in education must be beaten toward excellence. I believe in educators and in their capacity to accept good news without feeling that they don't need to improve.

In many ways I am one of public education's biggest critics. I believe it needs major transformation. The American dream still eludes far too many of our children. For those children from our bottom third economically, the chances for success are dismal. Poverty and racism still scar too many of our youngest and most vulnerable. For most of our children, the time they spend in school is too often full of boredom, glazed eyes, and numbed brains. We have much to do.

Let me be so bold as to say that the problem with America's schools is not that we have failed in our mission, but that we have done it too well. After the Industrial Revolution geared up, America needed workers for its factories. Public schools were created to act as the factories for the workers. Schools were asked to sort and match skills with needs. We became the best sorters of workers the world had ever seen. We still are. In fact, we keep getting better at it. We now are doing a fabulous job of educating children for the world of 1850, and a very good job of educating kids for the world of 1950.

Our institutional problem is that we are a better rearview mirror than we are a headlight. We are much more adept at reflecting the world and culture we already experienced than we are at anticipating and leading toward a new one. For that we deserve criticism.

A NOSTALGIC PERSPECTIVE

We do have many challenges and failures. However, they are not the ones that our critics bewail. Too many dropouts? Certainly in some portions of our society, particularly for children of poverty and color, dropping out of school is a problem. Yet we are graduating a greater portion of our population than ever before.

Today the price for dropping out is much stiffer. If you are not educated, you have no chance for a slice of the American pie. In 1950, you did have a chance, because the jobs did not require higher skill levels. You could make a good living by being very adept at repeating monotonous and simple actions on the assembly line.

Test scores down? Not really. When you consider the much broader pool of test-takers and the raised norms, we are doing fine. That is, if you really believe that tests mean anything in reflecting what children should know and that they really reflect what we have been teaching.

International comparisons? Should we really care how we compare to Singapore? Singapore is a city-state with a student population comparable to San Diego. It has a homogeneous society that brings service workers in every day from Malaysia and sends them home at night without worrying about educating the children of that class. Do not size, test sample, different curriculum, and different cultural assumptions and conditions come into play?

If you lean your ladder against the wrong wall, you paint the wrong house. Misdiagnosing what is wrong with schools today will lead us to cure the wrong disease. It appears that politicians and much of the press believe that you can bludgeon people to greatness—at least those working in public schools. It would appear that much of our current reform strategy is to beat people into being excellent. Guess what? It won't work.

MUCH TO CELEBRATE

Yes, you need greater skills today to do the same jobs. But a greater danger to America than our supposed deterioration of public education is that there are not enough good jobs available that pay a wage that allows for the American dream to be fulfilled. Even if you are well educated, there are not enough good jobs to go around. Competition for good jobs is up and wages are down, relative to the past.

No evidence exists that schools in the 1950s were better than they are today. Certainly, there was less crime in schools, as there was in society. There were fewer "hard-to-educate" children in school because we did not try to educate them. In truth, the golden age of the American economy was not about education. It was about having enough jobs to pay for our parents to buy into the American dream of owning their own home and putting two cars in the garage. This is a goal that will be much more difficult for our children, even if they get a great education.

There are many failures in our schooling process, but there are many successes and much we should celebrate. We have no room for complacency, but we have no reason to doubt our capacity for success. We must embrace a sense of efficacy that allows us to confront the challenges left undone and to ensure the continuation of the American dream.

23

VOUCHER ARGUMENTS BUILT ON SAND

Most of us remember Arnold Schwarzenegger's famous line from *The Terminator*: "I'll be back." Every time the voucher issue emerges, I think of *The Terminator*. Vouchers have proven to be persistent and impervious to destruction. They keep coming back.

By now we know the arguments against vouchers: they will hurt public schools by draining limited resources and by siphoning off middle-class children; they are not really parent-choice programs because it is the schools that get to choose, not the parents; the competitive playing field between private and public schools is not level since different rules apply to each; vouchers are not given to other areas of public service, such as fire or police protection; and schools fall into the area of vital public interest.

Certainly, no clear data have emerged to show that when like children are matched, vouchers do anything to improve learning. With so much logic arrayed against the idea, why then do vouchers have more lives than the Broadway cast of *Cats*?

First, we have to understand that there are two great emotions that drive human behavior—fear and trust. These emotions are intertwined. The more we fear, the less we trust, and vice versa. For a variety of reasons—some sound, some not—the public has increasingly come to fear and distrust public education.

Parents, in particular, have come to fear for their children's moral and physical safety. They assume that schools will not always act in their children's best interest.

This lack of trust and pervasive sense of fear have proven to be fertile ground for those who sing a siren song of choice and simple solutions to complex problems. One simple act could give people safety and peace of mind. If parents could get a voucher, schools would miraculously overcome the ravages of poverty, children would achieve at the levels of Singapore, and America would be great once more.

If only things were that simple. Lost in the discussion are the assumptions that underpin the voucher movement. Little has been said about them, yet logic tells us that the assumptions underpinning an argument must be sound for the argument to be sound. We learned as children that houses built on sand cannot withstand strong winds. The assumptions fueling the pro-voucher lobby will not be able to stand up to the strong wind of scrutiny.

First of all, vouchers will not be a lever to improve the "failed monopoly" of public education. The assumption that drives the belief that a market-driven approach will improve the system is that people working in schools are too lazy and uncaring to help children learn and that we will only get better through external pressure.

True, some people working in schools lack sufficient motivation—as do some people in the business community, media, or in the right-wing think tanks that espouse vouchers. But most care about doing a good job. Most of those working with children care deeply about their welfare. Their lack of success in helping some children achieve might be somewhat driven by other factors, such as poverty, lack of resources, and the breakdown of families and communities.

Despite difficult odds, though, some schools do heroic work. But heroism in life itself is not that common. That's why it is the basis of so many legends and fairy tales.

Secondly, education is not a private good. It is not owned by parents with the sole discretion over how that good is used.

Our great forefathers, who created public schools, were concerned about the common good. Children were to be educated not only for their own or their parents' benefit, but for the good of the country. That is why schools are governed by community members through committees and boards of education.

Certainly, it has not always worked as well as it should. There have been bad decisions made by school boards and superintendents. Our local control has led to local inequality. Some children have not been treated as they should. In short, it is a flawed and magnificently human undertaking—and it is very American in its structure and assumptions.

Now we are being asked to throw away that system for something wonderful in its simplicity and its wrong-headedness—a system in which everyone is on their own and the individual choice, paid for by everyone, is supreme.

Sorry. I do not pay taxes so someone can send their child, at my expense, to the David Koresh School of Marksmanship, or a Methodist (my religion), Moslem, Hebrew, or Catholic school, or to one that only teaches one narrow view of history, or that only accepts left-handed Presbyterians with IQs over 150. I pay taxes so that I can live in a society that has some common sense of responsibility and concern, and where we can appreciate, if only a little, the wonderful qualities our differences bring to the world.

Yes, we who are the stewards and servants of public education have much to do to make it better. We have to do better at educating those children who come to us unprepared. We have to do better at ensuring equal opportunity. We have to make schools places of joy and wonderment, instead of places of boredom and despair. We have to do it in a way that recognizes that our children are different and that one size does not fit all. We will have to do this in the face of dumb, destructive ideas such as vouchers that keep coming along.

We can start by helping people see the sand upon which such ideas are built.

Part IV

TRANSFORMING SCHOOL REFORM

When I first went to Washington, D.C., I was struck by the conversations on school reform and how little they had to do with the real world of the schools I had just left. In fact, one of my greatest fears was that as I became part of Washington, I would also become part of the disconnect between reality and expectations that has marked much of the school reform movement.

I have found this disconnect to be based upon bad assumptions about what the problems really are, mechanistic solutions to issues that are essentially organic in nature, a tendency to try to invoke learning instead of evoking it, and a perceived need to coerce people into compliance. None of these approaches comport with my experience or observations of what good education looks like.

I have stopped more than one meeting by suggesting that the best school reform would be to create schools that kids wanted to go to, and that school and joy are not polar ideas. I have come to believe that schools must be places where kids find meaning through engagement in the learning process.

It is ironic that the word *education* springs from the Latin word *educare*, which means "to draw forth." So much of so-called education reform is based on a model of pounding stuff into kids' heads instead of helping them create meaning from what they are doing.

I had a chance a couple years ago to speak to half of the United States Senate. I suggested I could save them a lot of money on student assessment. Of course, their ears perked up since most politicians love to hear the words "save money." I suggested that rather than testing our children, we simply go into classrooms and see which way they were leaning. If they were leaning forward you probably had a teacher there who had captured their hearts and minds. If they were leaning back in their seats, it was probably a pretty boring classroom, along the lines of the one depicted in *Ferris Bueller's Day Off*: "Anyone know what the laffer curve is? Anyone? Anyone?"

My friend Richard Farson has written about the paradoxes of leadership. One is that training makes people alike and education makes them different. Anyone know whether today's school reform is more training than education? Anyone? Anyone?

24

WHEN BAD THINGS HAPPEN TO GOOD IDEAS

My father always told me that confession is good for the soul. OK, I confess. I was one of the early advocates of the standards movement. It is ironic that such an admission makes me feel a little sullied. What started out as a wonderful idea now looks like an off-color joke. What happened to turn a noble idea into something that feels dirty?

Quite simply, the standards movement of today bears little resemblance to the concept that was once envisioned. For decades schools were asked to act as a sorting device for our society. We needed to separate out the talent and to place people in a hierarchical framework. And schools were great at it. As our society evolved, we came to realize the moral price we were paying for that kind of separation. As our economy evolved, we came to recognize the economic price extracted by wasting human capital. We realized everyone needed to be raised to a higher place.

The solution was simple: raise the standards and provide opportunity for everyone's boat to rise. The standards movement was a civil rights movement that saw everyone as deserving of the same opportunities. Higher standards for everyone meant greater opportunity for those who had been left behind. Create a clear set of expectations that would shape curriculum and assessment.

ENDLESS REQUIREMENTS

Today the standards movement has morphed into an amalgam of simplistic assessments tied to complex goals without adequate resources to meet them.

The victims of the movement are in many cases those very children it was created to save. They are the ones failing the tests and dropping out. Those punished by failure are the children we had wanted to empower. What happened to the good idea?

Two things occurred early on. One can clearly be laid at the feet of educators. Educators insisted that they be the ones to create the standards. The task was handed to the subject-area specialists. The outcome was predictable. The social studies folks thought social studies was the most important area and created massive lists of what kids should know in that area. This was repeated throughout the curriculum so that to meet the standards, children would have to stay in school many years past current graduation ages.

The community should have been more involved in setting standards—they are the ones whose values should embed education. What standards should a student meet to be a good citizen, a productive worker, and an upstanding family person?

Politicians created the other major problem. Everyone knew that for children who had not previously met the old standards to get to an even higher level, there must be dramatically increased resources to support them. The term "opportunity to learn standards" came to be discussed as the way to move resources—the opportunity to learn—alongside the new academic standards. But politicians almost immediately dismissed them. It was recognized that creating an equal opportunity would be very expensive. So expectations were raised, but very little was offered to help children meet them.

Some states, such as North Carolina and Texas, have had success in moving kids up in achievement. It is no accident that these are the two states that developed a comprehensive plan that included additional resources to support the higher standards.

ANSWERS FROM PRAYER

It is no mystery why poor children don't do as well in school as their more affluent peers. They don't have the same social capital given to them. They bring greater problems with them to the schoolhouse door—a door that in many cases leads to a classroom with fewer resources. For them to catch up, they must be given some of the same opportunities. If we insist on account-ability through high-stakes testing, then we must also insist that these children be given some of the same advantages that others have enjoyed for decades.

There are those who insist that you can't solve the educational problems by throwing money at them. If you look at the last forty years, we must acknowledge that during the 1960s and 1970s, we threw money at schools by increasing resources without insisting on accountability. During the 1980s and 1990s, we threw accountability at schools without a serious increase of resources. Perhaps we now have reached a point when we can all agree that accountability and resources must go hand in hand. Resources without accountability is foolish. Accountability without resources is cruel.

For the standards movement to reach its initial promise, we must realize that we are going to have to go back to the basics. We have to simplify the expectations and tie them more directly to the real world that the children will have to navigate. The assessments we give children will need to reflect that world, not merely be paper-and-pencil drills of filling in the bubbles. We will have to give those who aren't meeting the standards a lot more support before we hold them accountable for meeting a tougher set of expectations. Anything less means we all should go to confession and pray for our souls.

25

DIRTY SECRETS REVEALED!

The problem with the education reform movement is that we spend a lot of time and energy on ideas and actions that will not generate much return. We do that to avoid confronting issues that might be painful. This has led to a lot of dirty little secrets in education—things we all know but don't talk about.

Perhaps it's time to talk about those things so we can get on with real school improvement.

Secret number one: Size matters. Most of us know that schools are too big. We make them big to save money, provide more courses, and protect our athletic programs. Perhaps we should begin to pay attention to the research that shows smaller is better.

Administrators are trained from day one to protect economies of scale and the idea that bigger is more efficient. Bigger is also more impersonal and disconnected. It is no accident that the popularity of private schools, charter schools, and homeschooling is based on smallness. If we would stop building larger schools and begin breaking the ones we have into smaller units, we would find discipline improve, parental satisfaction increase, and even test scores go up.

Secret number two: We pay for education folks don't use. The first thing we should do is stop giving extra pay for master's degrees in administration or counseling to anyone who isn't actively involved in those jobs.

A significant portion of the master's degrees granted in education at present are in the fields of administration and counseling because most local school districts give extra salary credit for master degrees, regardless of field and whether those degrees are being used. Despite this plethora of degree recipients, there is a growing shortage of administrative candidates. The reality is that many people are getting degrees for salary purposes when they never intend to use them for anything else. And, sadly, the quality of many of these degrees is poor.

If school districts only gave salary credit for master's degrees in subject areas or teaching specialties, the quality of teaching actually might improve. People might start getting degrees in reading or math and who knows what educational improvements might result for children? And we could professionalize administration by raising our standards and focusing on those who are doing the work.

Secret number three: Most schools are dull and boring. So much of what we ask children to learn in school has little or no connection to them and their interests. They live in a world after school that is exciting and vibrant. During school, they learn things that someone else thinks will be good for them later. Schooling must be connected to doing.

This connection is the difference between belief, which is a feeling based upon what others tell us, and knowing, which is based upon our own experience. An old saying points out that if you "give a man a fish, he eats for a day, but teach him to fish and he eats for a lifetime." Giving is offering beliefs based upon reflected experience. Fishing is doing the work. It's time to take the kids fishing.

Secret number four: Teaching isn't a profession. There's a buzz in the air over the quality of teachers: where the new ones will come from, how professional they are, how much they are paid, and how they should be trained.

A simple but slightly costly answer to these questions exists. Put teachers on twelve-month contracts so they don't have to spend their summers painting houses or waiting tables. This would create a higher annual pay for teachers, making the profession more attractive and competitive. It also would allow districts to extend the school year for students and provide time for regular professional development that would not pull teachers away from their classrooms.

Creating a full work year for teachers would professionalize the role, add learning time for kids, and provide critical training.

The time has come for us to start uncovering our little secrets and shine some light into the dark corners of our profession. While we have much to be proud of and our critics are usually off base, there are things we should be ashamed of and be willing to change. That is called leadership.

26

A STAKE THROUGH THE HEART OF HIGH-STAKES TESTS

Confusion reigns among educators over the issue of high-stakes testing. Part of the problem is a lack of clarity over what is meant when we talk about it.

Let's be clear: developing and implementing higher standards for students and the adults who serve them is central to the future of education. This should be done thoughtfully and with a breadth that ensures we are educating our children, not merely training them. Students should be assessed regularly and broadly so that we know how they are doing and how we as educators are doing in serving their needs. Assessment should be keyed to improvement.

All of this should be tied together in a reasonable and realistic system of accountability, so that when things aren't working, they get changed. Anything less constitutes a failure in all of us.

However, all of this is far removed from the high-stakes testing movement that is now running rampant across the educational landscape. In short, high-stakes testing involves the use of a single measure, given at a single time that sets the future direction of a child's life. This is not just bad education, it is a major departure from the values of this country.

CLUELESS MEASURES

To enumerate the many reasons why the use of a single instrument to determine a child's future is a bad idea would take more space than I have in this brief chapter. Put at its simplest, high-stakes testing is a reductionist approach to learning that assumes that whatever is worth learning can be measured and, indeed, can be measured in one sitting. That is clearly a laughable assumption that, sadly, more than twenty states now are making.

Being an educated person constitutes many qualities for which we have no clues how to measure—creativity, honesty, and perseverance, among them. Even if everything worth knowing could be measured, it is clear we are not sophisticated enough at this point to have the instruments that would fairly and completely assess this knowledge. We also know that the variability issue is huge. Not only are there issues of test bias and test phobia, but we know that any one child's performance can vary dramatically day to day based on a host of circumstances.

The most telling educational argument against high-stakes testing comes from the cognitive scientists who point out that fear inhibits learning. High-stakes testing is perhaps the clearest example of an attempt to use blunt force to make children learn.

The logic is as follows: "If you don't pass this test, then you will have to stay in school all summer, be held back, not graduate, etc." I often refer to this approach as an attempt to bludgeon people to greatness. It never works. And cognitive scientists tell us why. When we go into a fear mode, much of our cerebral capacity is reduced. We enter that twilight zone of "fight or flight," and neither of these is particularly useful to the learning process. Certainly we must make sure children take the learning process seriously. We ought to be able to do that without making them sick to their stomachs and school phobic.

The other reason why high-stakes testing is a bad idea, whose time has come and needs to go, is that it is essentially un-American. One of the priceless values of our country is our bone-deep belief that where you come from should not keep you from going someplace better. We have been a country that believes in second chances. We always have been a country that understood the seeds of success are sown in failure. As my father, who was a Methodist minister, might have put it: we forgive people their trespasses.

SECOND CHANCES

When I speak to business groups on this, I love to ask how many of them would be doing what they are doing now if they had been held accountable for their actions at the age of thirteen. Hands never go up. We know that children develop at different rates and that each of us faces unique obstacles.

For us to be a fair nation, we needed to develop an educational system that took that into account. With all the faults and failings in our current model, it has been a system of second opportunities, a reflection of that very real American value of being able to pursue one's possibilities despite early failure. Other major developed countries followed a different model, in which students were tracked into different vocations at much earlier ages. That might be appropriate for places where social stratification is part of the culture, but it does not fit our American brand of egalitarian belief in the possibilities of the individual.

Richard Farson, author of *Management of the Absurd*, pointed out that training makes people alike and education allows them to be different. We, as a nation, must decide which path to travel. Making kids perform like trained seals at the demand of politicians might be entertaining, but it is not good education. Using a single test to determine a child's future is a lousy way to create educational improvement. It is even a worse way to educate an American.

27

VOUCHERS ARE ONE ENTITLEMENT WE CAN'T AFFORD

In case you haven't noticed, Washington is a funny place. Things do not mean the same thing here as they do in the real world. For example, most people know that dirty words usually have four letters.

In Washington, the dirty words are longer ones, like bureaucracy, welfare, regulation, and so on. Another is entitlement. Entitlement has come to mean all that is dirty in American life. Anyone who feels he or she is entitled to anything is suspect. This is the "land of the free and the home of the brave," and we are on our own. If you want something, you should get it the old-fashioned way— you should earn it.

This was made abundantly clear in discussions on welfare reform. It was widely agreed that our welfare system was broken and needed to be fixed. We set about ridding the nation of "welfare queens" who used the system to benefit from the hard work of others. Major changes in the laws were enacted to see to it that people went to work and stopped benefiting from the work of others.

The outcome has been dramatic. Aid to the poor has been reduced by billions of dollars. Aid to Families with Dependent Children is being block granted to the states, at reduced levels. States are allowed to divert funds formerly spent on the poor without penalty. The Urban Institute estimates that more than one million children have been pushed into poverty. This has significant social implications, but at least we will have made a huge dent in "entitlements."

At least that is what I thought until I visited New Zealand. While we were there, we talked with a member of parliament who also serves as a cabinet minister. New Zealand's majority party is conservative, and many of the ideas he shared with us sounded familiar to those heard daily on Capitol Hill. He raged on against the welfare state. He was quite concerned with the quality of education. His solution to education was vouchers. He averred that letting the marketplace loose on education would no doubt improve things. Competition would force the schools to work harder and provide better programs. This is all familiar territory for most of us. Then came the shock. Karl Hertz, the AASA president, asked him if he would give vouchers to the parents of children who were already in private schools and how he would pay for them.

He stopped, as if he had not really considered that before. He thought for a moment, and then said that he was not sure where the money would come from, but that it most certainly could be worked out.

I think one of the greatest concerns public school people have with vouchers is what the answer to this question will be. Most of us doubt that the money will come from anywhere but from what is currently going to education. This reallocation could wreak havoc in many communities.

But the real surprise came as he answered the first part of Hertz's question, "Would you give the money to those already in private school?" That caused him no pause at all, and I found his answer most surprising. He said, "Of course we would, it is an entitlement!" I could not believe it—a conservative politician using the dirtiest of words.

Of course, I should not have been too surprised. We are very comfortable with entitlements that go to the powerful and to those who already have. That is what home mortgage deductions and capital gains tax cuts are about. We provide entitlements to those who are perceived to have earned something, but deny them to those perceived as undeserving. Of course entitlement, like beauty, is in the eye of the beholder.

At any rate, the next time someone suggests to you that vouchers are a grand idea, tell them you are surprised that they would recommend a new entitlement program. It will not change their minds, but it will give them pause, and it will give you a moment of amusement.

Part V

SEEING AMERICA THROUGH A DISTANT MIRROR

One of the perks and perils of my job is the amount of time I spend on the road. When you are expected to be the visible and loud voice for a profession, you have to be out in the world to make the noise. But you must also understand the world to make some sense of it for those who can't be out there.

So much wisdom emerges merely from having some perspective. In addition to jetlag, bad food, security lines, and lost luggage, travel gives you perspective. It lets you see new worlds and old worlds through new eyes. Travel has always taught me a little bit about the places I see and a lot about the world I left at home. It has given me the hill to stand on so I can see the landscape more clearly.

As a poor preacher's kid from Davis Creek, West Virginia, it has sometimes astounded me that I have been to so many exotic places—places I saw in my fourth grade geography books but never thought I would see with my own eyes. And these places have given me perspective and understanding about others; but most of all, they have helped me understand myself. It has been my pleasure to share that with my readers.

I suppose what I have found to be universal is how beautiful children are. It doesn't matter which continent you are on, children are beautiful. They have that open-faced beauty that comes from not having had life step all over them just yet. It is the adults who have become hardened by life. And that is what we have to worry about.

I have also learned that while America is the richest country in the world, we don't necessarily value our children more—in fact, a case could be make

that relative to our capacity, we have much to learn from much more primitive cultures. While they may be thin in the pocketbook, they are rich in
spirit in the way they treat their children.

Of course, we have to be careful about comparisons. I have also found
that, despite criticism about our perceived failings, and despite the real
shortcomings we may have in our educational system, America's public
school system is still the envy of the world. And I have found that, while we
might pick up nuances from others, all education is culturally based, and
transfer of the system is almost impossible without buying the context as
well.

28

GOING WHERE
THE WATER IS

On a trip to Eastern Europe, our study group was visiting yet one more museum when our guide started talking about a series of kings, all of whom were assassinated. She ended her little talk with the thought, "That was a bad time to be a king." I couldn't help but think about the times our educational community now faces, and the feeling we often get is that this is a bad time to be an educator.

Certainly we are under immense pressure to create results without sufficient resources and to provide accountability without authority. We are scrutinized, vilified, and occasionally crucified for our efforts. But as the thought goes, "Tough times don't last, but tough people do." These are truly the times when we have to dig down and make things happen despite the challenges.

While on that same trip, we were taking a riverboat ride along the Danube. As the tour guide was explaining the workings of the boat, one passenger asked if they used a global positioning system, or GPS, for navigation. The guide replied, "When you are on the river, you don't have to know where north is, you just have to know where the water is."

NEWFOUND APPRECIATION

What a wonderful bit of guidance for us as we navigate turbulent times. Sometimes we spend so much time trying to gather data and information that we get stuck in what management gurus call "analysis paralysis." We know so much we can't move. Yet what we have to do is focus on following the course of the water, avoiding the sandbars, and seeking the center channel where the water runs deeper and safer. And while we are watching for hazards, we shouldn't forget to take in the view.

Several years ago when I was diagnosed with an eye condition that if left untreated would threaten my sight, I noticed an immediate change in myself. I started paying attention to things. I noticed the sunsets. I looked at the hills and trees with new eyes. I not only stopped to smell the roses, I really looked at them. You never appreciate something until you are threatened with losing it.

Well, given the pressures on public education, we are facing real and grave threats. Now is the time for us to appreciate what public education offers and to share that appreciation with others. Public education is messy, imprecise, inefficient, and falls far short of the dreams we all have for it. But it is also the one institution that holds our democracy together and offers dreams to our children.

Later on the trip, we were visiting a school outside of Prague, where the principal explained to us that he had been the principal there in the early 1970s. He left education for nearly twenty years and had returned to the school in the early 1990s to resume his work. He noted that he had left for political reasons. He said, "[The communists] wanted me to teach things that were not true. And they wanted me not to teach things that were, so I had to make a choice."

Good leadership is always about making that moral choice to lead toward the truth and to overcome the darkness of deceit.

A RESCUE MISSION

On the way home, I was seated on the plane next to several gentlemen from Great Britain. One was a firefighter from a small village in eastern England, who on the days just after September 11th had gone around his village raising money for the families of New York City firefighters. He had raised more than $20,000 for those families and he was flying to New York (accompanied by a TV camera crew) to present the check to the fire chief.

I asked him why he had made such an effort on behalf of people he didn't know. He looked at me with the same look of bewilderment that I saw on the face of our tour guide when asked about the boat's need for a global positioning system. The firefighter said, "I had no choice. I had to do it. They would have done it for me."

It struck me that the firefighter and the principal from Prague both offered me the moral equivalent of a GPS for leaders in tough times. When it comes to questions of morality and principle, you must make a choice. You must choose to stand up and do what's right. And I believe if you are a leader of principals, you have no choice but to do what's right. That is truly understanding where the water is and following the right channel in the river.

Just after the British firefighter told me that he had had no choice but to help his peers in New York, one of his companions asked me, "What, didn't you do that too?"

I'll leave that question with each of you. Every day, we face a search-and-rescue mission for our children. What choices are you making?

29

LESSONS FROM
THE AMAZON

As our group bumped along the rutted road taking us to the boat that would be home for the next week, we strained our eyes to pierce the dark undergrowth for a first glimpse of the Amazon River. Once the bus stopped, we walked across a rickety dock to approach La Tourmalina, our home for the next few days. We rushed on deck for our first real glance of the great Amazon, a river we had known in our imagination and from our fourth grade geography lessons.

And there it was, stretching almost as far as the eye could see, snaking off almost infinitely into the moonlight—home to headhunters, anacondas, and piranhas. The Amazon is more than a river; it is a spark to imagination that stirs the spirit of adventure. And now, here I was, ready for a week of taking it all in.

The trip was an opportunity to see the rainforest—the lungs of the earth—while it was still there. The vibrant plant life churns out a major portion of the world's supply of oxygen, and now greed for another form of green was destroying thousands of its acres every day. The trip afforded me the opportunity to learn about the fragile ecology and the need for maintaining our biodiversity so that new cures for disease may come from the ancient plants found in the jungle. But I learned much more.

As we churned upriver, we passed the primitive villages of the natives. They looked just like what my almost-forgotten elementary geography books described—huts built on stilts with grass roofs and no sides. As we docked at different villages and visited, we found the people friendly, eking out a pre-agrarian existence. They survived by hunting and gathering.

Their lifestyle was in tune with the environment, and they suffered little from the diseases that kill citizens of the developed world. They die from infections and lack of sanitation.

Each village had a school, usually a ramshackle tin structure in the middle of the village. Certainly they were not the kinds of buildings we send our children to. But then everything is relative. These structures were the best buildings in the village. If it takes a village to raise a child, then those villagers had figured out that their children deserved the best of what they could provide.

It struck me that most of our schools are far from the best buildings in our towns and that we had something to learn from these so-called primitive people.

WHOSE CONTROL?

Another lesson came from watching the power of the river at work. It would eat away huge chunks of riverbank, with massive trees falling and being swallowed up by the restless water. As we watched this display, we thought that if this river were back in America, the U.S. Army Corps of Engineers would be hustling in to spread acres of concrete along the bank to hold the river back. We asked the boat crew what they did to control the river, and they just looked at us. "Sir, the river goes where it will" was the bemused reply.

What a powerful lesson! The river goes where it will. As we educators face the uncertain future of deregulation, the devolution of power to dispersed corners, and the fragmented society that we see developing, we are busy building dikes against the flood—not understanding that ultimately the river goes where it will.

The people who live along the Amazon River don't fight it, they accommodate it. They take what the river offers in food and supplies. They use it as their highway. They literally have learned to "go with the flow." Would we as people in the developed world be better served if we took a leaf from their forest?

FRUITLESS SEACHING

We learned another lesson the day we went in search of dolphins. The Amazon River is home to the only freshwater dolphins on earth. And they are pink! We went off in a small boat to see them. After several hours of fruitless searching, no dolphins were to be seen. We made our way back to the Tourmalina and settled in for the evening. The next morning I awoke to sounds of splashing beside the boat. When I went out I found the boat surrounded by dozens of cavorting bright pink dolphins. They had found us.

So much of the time in our business we spend searching fruitlessly for the right answer to our problems. We go on "pink dolphin" chases in search of the elusive solution, when if we would relax, often it will come to us. I believe that in the future much of the education of our children will come to them, rather than children going somewhere to get it. We in the business must learn that our jobs will be as river guides to help them navigate the great muddy waters successfully—not to try to damn up the river and to control the environment. The river goes where it will and so will they.

30

A SENSE OF
DIRECTION IN THE
TRUE NORTH

In 1999, I visited the northernmost school district in North America, the North Slope District in Barrow, Alaska. I was there at the invitation of one of our members, Leland Dishman, a dynamic and unorthodox superintendent who created excitement serving the more than two thousand students who are stretched across a district about the size of Nebraska.

The North Slope gives a whole new meaning to the words *rural* and *isolated*. This trip, coming as it did a week before my excursion to Capetown, South Africa, allows me to claim legitimately that I go to the ends of the earth for my members. But the trip to Barrow was about much more than bragging rights.

Barrow, which is the township center and the home of the school district's headquarters, sits beside the Arctic Sea at the very edge of North America. Watching the Arctic waves roll in, I realized I was in a place where time slows down. The pace of daily life is gentler and the concerns more basic. During my visit to the edge of the earth, I realized that the edges are where things happen. I was also reminded that life as most of us know it is not how life is for the rest of the world.

FULL-TIME DEDICATION

In our rush to the mall or to get through traffic, we lose sight of the fact that most of the world has no cars and that for many one store is a lot. But it has been my experience that those who live a more basic life are often more in touch with life's essentials. Barrow was no exception.

I was struck by the dedication of the teachers and administrators to their work and to their children. School for them is a full-time job. When you teach in one of the North Slope villages, you are there for the winter. The school is the center of the community, and the kids come and go throughout the evening. Being a slave to city luxuries, I asked them what they found to do to occupy their time, and they told me their lives were so full with the work and the children they had little extra time to worry about it.

Dishman and his staff molded an exciting learning environment for their Eskimo children. Fortunately, the North Slope is blessed with oil reserves, so resources are available to offset the isolation that surrounds the children. The staff takes advantage of every kind of technology to expose the children to the wider world. They also bring in outside experts to spark children's interest.

My trip coincided with a visit by three NASA astronauts, whom the district had brought in to enrich the children's experience. I went around with the astronauts to visit classes and watch them interact with the children. It was stunning to see the children use the technology of televised distance learning, to interact with the astronauts about space travel, and then to hear the children discuss going out after school with their parents in skin-covered boats to hunt whales, just as their ancestors had done for thousands of years.

My head was spinning, but the children didn't seem the least bothered by that paradox. I also was struck that in this age of school safety concerns, one of the biggest safety issues for the North Slope is helping the kids learn how to avoid polar bear attacks. Here I was, at the end of the millennium, visiting a world in which many of the issues were as old as time itself. The children had to have a foot in each of the worlds of past and future, and they moved between these worlds effortlessly.

DISTANT DISCOVERIES

Isn't that really what education is about? Aren't we about helping our children honor the past and navigate the future? Aren't we about helping them explore the stars while keeping their feet firmly planted on the ground? And isn't our task about giving our children everything we have to give and to live every day as we would live it on the edge?

As you fly over the villages on the North Slope, one building always stands out in stark relief—the school. Yet today the value of our public school system is often overshadowed by other issues, and this oversight carries enormous repercussions. I have come to believe that in many ways our society is on the edge—on the edge of losing our way as a democracy, on the edge of losing our understanding of which way true north lies, and on the edge of abandoning our village of common concern for each other.

The one institution that stands in the way of losing all that, of succumbing to a vicious attack of polar bears, if you will, is our public school system. In today's climate of school reform, high-stakes testing, and accountability, it is easy to lose sight of the reason education exists—to help the next generation find their wider world. That's what my visit to Barrow reminded me.

Near the end of my last day there, I spotted a quote from Andre Gide hanging on the wall of one of the schools that I thought should be on every school leader's wall. Gide, the Nobel Prize-winning French author, reminded us that "one doesn't discover new lands without consenting to lose sight of the shore for a very long time."

Education is about helping our children learn to navigate the world, so that the trip of discovery away from the edge of the shore is a safe and successful journey.

31

NAVIGATING DANGEROUS WHITE WATER TOGETHER

I have often felt that the best training for a school leader would involve an Outward Bound experience culminating with white-water rafting. Think about it. We spend most of our time navigating turbulent water. Those who surround us are in the same boat, dependent on each other for support and encouragement. If the boat springs a leak, we all get wet. Through it all are the rapids and towering rocks.

One interesting thing about the boats we spend our time in—the schools, systems, and communities where we work—is that so many of them encompass people who want to punch holes in the bottom of the boat. It is not enough that the world outside poses danger. These people add to it by creating damage and danger from their own actions.

What is crazy is they fail to realize that their actions endanger themselves as well. Yet selfishness, racism, narrow-mindedness, and blind ambition are all little daggers poised over the fragile covering of our boats. These issues do not only hurt others; they hurt the ones holding the dagger. One role we as leaders must play is to help disarm people and keep them from hurting themselves and others by giving them a vision of the whole.

We have to help people work together. It is important to remember that everyone in the boat has a job to do that is critically important. Sometimes you do the same thing, all rowing forward to propel the boat down the river. But that can change.

The day I went rafting, I found that as we approached a rapid, everything changed. The people seated on one side of the boat rowed forward, while those seated on the other side rowed backwards. We did this to align the boat so we could hit the center of the rapid. If we did that, we would shoot right through to the calm water beyond the rapids. If we failed in this collaborative, synergistic activity, we had one of two bad experiences. Either the boat flipped, dumping all of us into the icy water, or the boat spun around and went through the rapid backward. That gave us a great view of where we had been, but no idea of where we were headed.

We, too, are navigating some dangerous white water. We face many hidden boulders and swirling, choppy waters. It would be wise of us to remember that we are in the boat together and if one of us gets wet, we all get wet. We have to look out for each other. Our common schools were created to do that for America. Our role as leaders is to create that sense of common purpose in our institutions and in our communities. It was important. Now it is critical.

As we become a more pluralistic nation, we must find ways to create solidarity out of our differences. We can compete with each other for resources or we can complement each other. We can battle for scraps or we can help one another find greater abundance by sharing.

Most of us are familiar with the biblical story of the loaves and the fish. A large crowd had gathered. It was time to eat and there was no food. Everyone was asked to give what they had. A young boy had brought lunch (probably packed by his mother). It was only five loaves and two fish, yet somehow when it was divided, it was enough to feed everyone.

Our usual understanding of the story is that a miracle occurred. That much was created from little. However, I think the miracle of the story was not what was done with the food. The real miracle was what the people did for each other. It was not in the division of the food, but in the multiplication that their openness and generosity created.

Creating a sense of common good is the way to create abundance from scarcity. Those kinds of miracles are available to us every day if we can find ways to set aside our self-interest and seek the common good.

We can operate out of a sense of self and a worldview of scarcity or we can join together to find abundance. We can go it alone or we can go it together. That is what common schools are really all about. That is what the American dream symbolizes—going down the road together, with a sense of common destiny. Helping people down that road is the most important thing any of us will ever do.

32

PLAYING
UP LEARNING,
NOT SCORES

It is always good to reflect on the gifts we receive. I have been given many opportunities by representing educational leaders. One of these has been the ability to travel internationally and to gain insights from this travel.

Insight one: There is a limit to what you can learn from other countries.

While you can gain new approaches from other countries, it is dangerous to think that we can borrow wholesale from them. America is huge compared to other countries. For example, we hear a lot about the great job Singapore is doing educationally. However, its student enrollment is about the size of San Diego City Schools. The complexity of our society, with its diversity of income levels, ethnic groups, and twenty-first century economy, makes comparisons with others fairly useless. Cultures are very different, which makes borrowing from other countries difficult to do. We worry about child abuse, but in Singapore caning is used as a form of punishment.

Insight two: America is educationally better than we think.

Trashing American public education has become a national pastime. It is difficult to find a layperson who does not believe that American schools are dismal. Yet, when you visit other countries, you find that in many ways we do a better job educating our children than they do. Certainly our interest in educating all children leads the world. I am struck by those in other countries who are open in their admiration for our system and who want to emulate what we are doing. We do have serious challenges, but it would be useful to keep our challenges and our successes in some perspective.

Insight three: Children seem to matter more elsewhere.

Regardless of whether I have been in a former communist country, a third world country, or countries similar to ours, children seem to count in those countries more than they do here. Even in the poorest place, you will find that adults revere their children and pin their hopes on them. In America, our public policies tell a different story. We lag behind in offsetting the effects of poverty and in ensuring adequate health care and children's rights. If we really want to be first in the world in learning, we should consider becoming first in the world in our treatment of children.

Insight four: Bad ideas know no borders.

Nearly every place I have been, I run into some of the same dumb ideas I left at home—like vouchers. New Zealand, whose public schools are already a charter system, has politicians pushing for vouchers. You have to wonder if there isn't a "Stupid Idea Handbook for Politicians" that is required reading all over the world.

Insight five: The best accountability is the least accountability.

I have noticed that those schools that seemed to be the most exciting for children, and where the most learning was taking place, were also places that did not worry much about test scores. They were very concerned about what their parents and communities thought about their children's schooling. In Australia, it is against the law to use test scores to compare schools. Tests are used to inform instruction, not to compare children or schools. What a radical idea!

Insight six: The best education is the most child centered.

I was very excited to find that the schools in New Zealand were truly places where children wanted to be. There was great joy among the children and relaxation among the teachers. Children helped each other and demonstrated independence and self-directed learning. Student projects were evident; textbooks were not. Yet, it seemed that the children were doing the work and the teachers were facilitating. Often in our schools, the teachers work and the children watch.

Insight seven: Learning takes courage.

In New Zealand, several of us visitors bought the sheepdog whistles that are used by farmers to direct their dogs to herd sheep. Everyone who got a whistle soon learned to get a peep out of it. Within a day, they were getting a variety of sounds, and by day two, they were playing songs. Everyone but me. I huffed and I puffed, but I could not get anything out of the whistle but spit. This went on for three days. Finally, I got a peep. In a few minutes, I produced a number of sounds. Within a couple of hours I was doing "Ode to Joy," not only because I could, but because that was how I felt. I was overjoyed to get the dog whistle monkey off my back. How many of our kids are out there right now, huffing and puffing, trying to master something that others make look easy? How often do we forget that different people learn in different ways and on different schedules? It takes guts to keep trying to learn, particularly when your first efforts meet failure.

Insight eight: In looking at others, we learn more about ourselves than we learn about them.

Every time I return home from a trip, I realize that while I learned a little about the country I visited, I learned a lot more about America. Our challenge is to make America's schools places of joy, and America a place that values its children. If so, we will all have found a way to play "Ode to Joy"—dog whistle or not.

33

VIEWING TEACHERS, STUDENTS, AND SCHOOLS AS INDIVIDUALS

In 1997, I had the opportunity to visit New Zealand and I found the visit instructive. New Zealand, while it shares some of our common heritage, is very different from the United States. It is much smaller, much more homogeneous, and it shares more of the good manners found in England than the free-spiritedness in the United States. Further, it is always easier to see what is good about another place and to overlook what might be a problem. With these cautions in mind, I did see some things that I thought were worth considering.

First, I have always felt that despite the criticisms leveled at American schools, we had one major advantage—we were educating the most creative, free-spirited group of children on the face of the globe. This is what I thought until I visited classrooms in New Zealand. The children in New Zealand make American kids look absolutely stifled. They are spontaneous, creative, collaborative, and alive. The classrooms were buzzing with activity and what some might mistake for chaos. Yet, if you observed individual children, it was apparent that they were productively engaged, happy to be where they were, and behaving independently. I do not pretend to know why or how this was achieved, but I found some clues.

Teachers in New Zealand act as facilitators rather than fountains of knowledge. A teacher is a "guide on the side" and not a "sage on the stage." When you enter a classroom, it is sometimes hard to find the teacher. They are working with individuals or small groups while the rest of the class is working independently or in small groups. Ironically, the teachers are less trained than teachers in the United States, with many having only a couple of years of college. Perhaps this allows them to see themselves as a part of the learning process, rather than the source of knowledge.

There are relatively few textbooks in the classroom. Learning seems to be centered on smaller workbooks and student- and teacher-created materials. This allows for more spontaneity and flexibility. Students are not being marched through a prescribed curriculum. This not only is less costly, but it seems to free the students and teachers.

There is a lot of emphasis on different ages working together. I saw a lot of tutoring and students helping other students. We have known for some time that there is much to be gained from student tutoring programs. However, the age segregation practiced in American schools seems to block our extended use of what the research tells us. The informality of the classrooms in New Zealand allows them to escape this lock-step approach.

Schools are not sued in New Zealand. I was immediately struck in my visit by the sight of children and teachers going barefoot. Then at recess the teachers retreated to the lounge for tea, and the children went outside unsupervised. The teachers busy themselves with discussing educational and classroom issues, and the children play. When we asked about their concerns over liability, they stated that schools could not be sued and that it was not an issue. This is not a readily transferable concept, but it did bring to mind the quote from Shakespeare, who said, "First let's kill all the lawyers." If not kill, at least there is something to be said for keeping them away from the learning process. I observed no problems and no injuries, but I did see lots of laughter and play.

Schools in New Zealand are basically all charter schools. There is a centralized authority in New Zealand for set educational goals, but each school does its own curriculum and is run by a locally elected board. The board is elected by the parents of the local school and makes most of the spending and educational decisions. The role of administrator is a tricky one there also. One of the principals described himself as feeling like a "piggy in the middle," which I thought well captured the role of administrators all over the world. The principals have plenty of latitude, but they work for the boards. The principals bemoaned the increased administrative responsibilities they had, but none of them wanted to go back to the more centralized approach. Additionally, they all seemed to have a good working relationship with their parent communities. Witnessing these things made me reassess my thinking on charters.

Funding is based on student need. Schools are funded by a formula that accounts for poverty. The poorer the school, the better the funding. Despite our own wars in the United States over equity in school funding, in New Zealand it is a nonissue. Everyone seems to accept and understand that kids who come to school with problems need more support to overcome them, and it is in everyone's best interest to see that this happens.

As we visited their classrooms, we noticed the world maps that are ubiquitous in classrooms. We noticed that the center of their map is the Pacific Ocean, and New Zealand is in the center of that area. We were a bit hurt to see that the United States was way off in the right corner of the map. It reminded me that we all feel that we are the centers of our universe. Yet we are not. We are just one part of the map, and we all have things we can learn from other quarters.

Part VI

AT THE MOVIES

Movies and television have always fascinated me. I grew up wanting to make movies. What I have found interesting is that I have run across other superintendents who have had the same thoughts. Perhaps the dreamers in us found magic in trying to transform lives, so that while we did not direct one kind of drama, we came to be centered in one much more real and with higher stakes.

I have also found that movies are powerful when the stories they tell are powerful. In the movie *Grand Canyon*, Steve Martin plays a movie producer who explains to one of the characters that movies have everything in them that life has, and so we can all relate to them.

Movies are also useful to write about because they create a common experience that allows us to bridge one idea to others. They open windows to the world of understanding and let all of us see things we wouldn't otherwise. That's why I go to the movies. At least, that's my story, and I'm sticking to it!

34

THE GLADIATOR
IN ALL OF US

I love movies. They take us away from where we are to lands and times far, far away. They are a great escape. They also bring us the truth that only can be found in fiction by focusing our attention on the stories and metaphors that reveal the deeper truths that undergird the fantasy.

One of my favorite recent movies is *Gladiator*. It depicts a fictionalized account of Maximus, a Roman general who, because of his integrity and loyalty to the Emperor Marcus Aurelius who is murdered and succeeded by his son, is thrown into slavery by the emperor's son and then becomes one of Rome's greatest gladiators.

There is much in this movie for a school administrator to ponder. First is the metaphor of the gladiator as school leader. Gladiators are warriors. They take their place in the center of the coliseum where they are pitted against all sorts of dangers and challenges. They are forced to fight it out in public—in fact for the entertainment of the public. When the fight is ended, the audience gives them the thumbs up or the thumbs down. Live or die. Any superintendent can relate to that moment. How many times do we face that awful moment of truth? After we have given our all to the fray, the public then judges us, sometimes in a circus-like atmosphere. If we entertained them acceptably, we live. If not, the sword falls.

Likewise, we are immersed in an era in which the educational landscape is dotted with the tendency toward thumbs-up and thumbs-down decisions concerning our children. Zero-tolerance policies, high-stakes testing, and high standards supported with inadequate resources are all thumbs-down rulings that can kill our children's dreams.

A related feeling comes early in the movie when Maximus, who is commanding the Roman legions in the war in Germania, tells his officers, "At my command, unleash hell." Maximus, at that moment, was aware of his awesome power to destroy. Maximus would have made a great school leader. Not because he had the capacity to unleash hell, but because he had the self-awareness to know that he was doing so. I'm afraid that the reason some of us face the moment when we receive the thumbs down is because we don't have the self-knowledge of how we are affecting those around us.

UPLIFTING ACTIONS

Those of us in leadership positions, because of our influence over others, have the capacity to create a living hell for those in our organizations. We can, by bullying and by manipulating, create an atmosphere in which spirits are stifled and destroyed. Our jobs require a sense of toughness. We must make hard decisions. But we shouldn't become hard in the process. Otherwise, we unleash hell on our own troops and our own children.

One of the gentler ironies in the movie is that throughout, even though death and destruction (a living hell) surround Maximus, his thoughts and dreams are on Elysium, the Roman version of heaven. Without getting overly theological, the reality is that there is both heaven and hell here on earth and we are the ones who create it. Leadership is about uplifting and affirming those around us. It is about planting the fields of Elysium for those in our charge.

One scene that was particularly instructive involved Maximus, who, along with a band of other gladiators, is sent to the center of the coliseum. They are there to be sacrificed in a spectacle in which the favored gladiators would ride out in chariots and decimate the hapless slaves. Maximus tells the other sacrificial warriors that the only way they can survive is to stand together. They do stand together and destroy the larger and better equipped opponents, thereby upsetting the expectations of the crowd.

The work we do often is lonely work, and we feel isolated in the center of the arena. However, nothing that we do can be accomplished successfully without working with others. We have to teach our staff and our community to work together to overcome the odds and to upset the expectations. By helping them stand back to back and shoulder to shoulder, we can overcome even the most daunting dangers. Going alone ensures our own destruction and the failure of the organization.

CARETAKER ROLE

The most powerful moment in the movie for me, and the most important for a school leader to think about, came when one character asks another, "What is Rome?" The answer was clear and concise: "Rome is an idea."

We could ask ourselves that same question today, "What is America?" And the answer is the same: "America is an idea." And we, as the caretakers of the last vestige of common civic purpose in this democracy, which was founded on the ancient principles that the people share a common bond, are the keepers of that idea.

For America to survive as a place of freedom requires that the people stand together. The common schools of this country are the one place that we can still experience the sense of common purpose with those who are different from ourselves. And for America to survive, we must give our children a chance at their Elysium by nurturing their dreams. That is a very powerful role for us to play, and truly a thumbs-up mission for each of us.

35

BOMBING CHILDREN
INTO THE STONE AGE

Last spring, one of the television networks showed the movie *Failsafe* as a live performance. *Failsafe* was written at the height of the Cold War and featured a confrontation between Russia and the United States that ended in the United States accidentally launching missiles at Moscow. To prevent a full-scale nuclear war, the American president agreed to drop nuclear bombs on New York City as a sign of good faith to Russia to prove that we were not interested in starting World War III.

The movie is a disturbing view of our history and a moral lesson of how close humanity can come to societal suicide. If we use *Failsafe* as a metaphor for our current approach to educational improvement, we see similar disturbing overtones.

For years public education has been under threat. Some even suggest a conspiracy is operating to destroy public education. Beginning with *A Nation at Risk*, America has been told its public schools are failing and that drastic action is needed. In fact, that report pointed out that if this failure had been imposed on us by a foreign power, it would be considered an act of war. While those of us in schools understand that the rhetoric was overblown and the accusations of failure were exaggerated, we also know we are not doing all we should for all our children.

Improvement must be made much faster now than in the past. Further, today's economy demands higher skills, even in formerly low-skill jobs. That means we can no longer tolerate some of our kids doing well and some not.

The needs of the changing workplace are one reason behind the standards movement and the current emphasis on testing to those standards.

MINDING THE GAP

Now let me strike while the irony is hot. The whole school reform movement is built on the assumption that we must bring all our children to higher standards. It could be convincingly argued that many of our kids are already there. Most children who go to schools in middle-class or affluent areas have adequate skills for the current workplace, and many of them have higher skills than their future jobs will demand. However, children who go to school where there are concentrations of poor children tend to have a more difficult time. Efforts at improvement, by definition, are aimed at those children, since they are the ones not meeting the standards. In essence, the whole standards movement targets poor children as its ultimate goal.

Yet the system that has been devised to help them seems singularly inappropriate to the task. The theory behind higher standards is that holding lower expectations for these children is racist and will hold these children back from future success.

This is true, but a difference exists between expectations and standards. Standards are somewhat arbitrary external creations of what someone else thinks someone else should do. Expectations are internal manifestations of what a person comes to believe about what they should do for themselves. Developing higher expectations for low-income kids is appropriate. But standards arbitrarily developed by others are too often disconnected from children's lives.

Now we lay on top of that a high-stakes test that says that in one fell swoop we will determine not only whether students have mastered the standards but also whether they are capable of moving to the next step in the process. It is a perverse form of Monopoly that says that if they pass the test, they can pass Go and collect their reward. Fail and they are held back in jail. Again, the brunt of these tests is aimed at poor children. Middle-class children can pass them.

All this might make some sense if we provided resources to the targeted children to prepare them for these attacks. If low-income children had higher per-pupil support, the best teachers, the finest facilities, and great curriculums, all this might make sense. But we know that is rarely the case. So we are targeting the very children who get the least to shoulder the heaviest burden. They are the victims of the system we have created.

CREATING THE MEANS

This brings me back to *Failsafe*. While we can blame governors and state legislators who are ignorant about education or who have failed to correct the inequities over which they preside, the educational leaders are constructing the accountability systems that lead to the destruction of some of our children.

Educators are doing that out of political expediency, to prove we can be accountable. While we did not create the ends, we are the architects of the means. In essence, we are creating educational systems that are bombing some of our children back to the Stone Age so that we can preserve the public education system for the rest. We can protest that "the devil made us do it," but our silence and acquiescence marks us for responsibility. We are the ones sacrificing one city so the others may live. While this might be politically smart and helpful to our own survival, I am not sure it is conscionable.

Yes, we must be accountable to the public. Yes, we must raise the bar for all children and most especially for those at the bottom. But we have to give them the support necessary to survive. They must be given shelter. If we are going to go down the path to higher standards and high-stakes testing, we must make certain that those who are targeted fall under an umbrella of support and safety that is our responsibility to provide. Anything less from a school leader is no profile in courage.

36

LIBERATING MINDS AND SPIRITS

Years ago there was a movie about African lions called *Born Free*. The movie followed the lions in their natural environment. On a recent trip to Kenya, as we bounced across the vast Masai Mara on the northern end of the Serengeti searching for the next pride of lions, I found myself humming the theme song from that movie: "Born free, as free as the grass grows, as free as the wind blows, born free to follow your heart." And then I found myself thinking of our children and the education we give them.

On the savanna, life is rich, complex, and fluid. There is nothing more magnificent than animals in the wild. They are sleek, healthy, and free. In fact, I think it is their freedom that makes them sleek and healthy. The natural order of life is at work there. The animals move to their own rhythm and rhyme. They compete and collaborate in a totally natural way.

As we pulled up next to them in our land rovers, it was clear we were the intruders. We were in the cages and they were free. There is something exhilarating about freedom, which is probably why so many wars have been fought for it and so many have been willing to die to preserve it.

CONFINING STRUCTURES

Think with me about how we approach learning. We take our children, who are magnificent in their freedom, and we put them into containers with others. We take control of their time and try to control their minds. And then we move

---

them to another container and another keeper. We make them sit still and be quiet—totally unnatural acts for healthy five-year-olds (or fifty-year-olds, for that matter!). And if they get too restless, we suggest they control themselves or, as Archie Bunker used to suggest to Edith, "to stifle."

As our nation has rushed precipitously toward common standards and high-stakes assessment, we have built even stronger and more constricting containers. Now it is not just children's behavior, but also what and how they learn that must be controlled. All those things that might be natural to children, such as the joy of movement and creative expression, are being squeezed out of the curriculum so that a common set of intellectual learnings can take place.

And we test their performance. Here the image shifts from zoo to circus. We place them in the center ring, shine the spotlight on them, and demand they jump through hoops. With the advent of high stakes, we have set the hoops on fire, and if they get singed, we make them jump through again.

At some point, we must recognize that natural is better than artificial; that reality is superior to virtual; and that, above all, a balance is better than an overemphasis on only one thing, that performance on a test is no substitute for the real world.

Yes, we must challenge their minds, but do so with meaningful challenges—not artificial activities that act as surrogates for the real thing. And while we challenge their minds, we also must address the needs of their hearts and souls. Otherwise our attempts at fixing their minds could become like the lobotomy performed on McMurphy in *One Flew over the Cuckoo's Nest*. He became docile and controllable. But when they took out his baser impulses, they also lobotomized his spirit. We must make sure we let our children's spirits run free.

The ancient wisdom of Taoism, which comes from the Far East, suggests that water is stronger than rock because it is fluid and can wear the rock away. That which moves trumps that which is stagnant. In tropical climates, one avoids standing water, for therein lies the beginnings of disease and death. It is only that which moves and is free that provides life. We must make certain that our education is fluid and flowing and unconstricted.

Movement is energy. Energy is life. When energy is contained, it builds up and ultimately explodes. Is it any wonder that we have to worry about violence with our children? When we contain their energy, we create an explosive potential in them. Or, perhaps just as sadly, we kill their spirit and their will to be active, creative people. And that may be a greater violence.

REMOVING SHACKLES

Education is about putting shackles on children's worst impulses, but it also should be about freeing their minds and liberating their spirits. Education should be about channeling their energy, not containing it. Children are born free. Our task is to let that freedom blossom into a life that is rich with the promise of possibilities.

Education isn't about setting limits. It's about widening horizons. It's about letting children see the world in all its breadth and beauty. Education, at its core, is about creating freedom—freedom of thought and action.

As we look at improving education, let's spend as much time worrying about that as we do worrying about test scores. The ultimate act of education is not about following directions. It is about following dreams.

ABOUT THE AUTHOR

Paul D. Houston, who has served as executive director of the American Association of School Administrators since 1994, has established himself as one of the leading spokespersons for American education through his extensive speaking engagements, published articles and books, and regular appearances on national radio and television. He worked in schools in North Carolina, New Jersey, and Alabama prior to serving as superintendent of schools in Princeton, New Jersey; Tucson, Arizona; and Riverside, California.